THE
RHYMESTER:
OR,
THE RULES OF RHYME.

A GUIDE TO ENGLISH VERSIFICATION.
WITH
A DICTIONARY OF RHYMES,
AN EXAMINATION OF CLASSICAL MEASURES, AND
COMMENTS UPON BURLESQUE, COMIC VERSE,
AND SONG-WRITING.

BY THE LATE TOM HOOD.

EDITED, WITH ADDITIONS, BY
ARTHUR PENN.

Tom Hood

Tom Hood was born in Leytonstone, London, England in 1835. He attended Pembroke College, Oxford, where he studied for the Church and passed all the examinations required for his Bachelor of Arts, but didn't graduate. While at university he wrote his *Farewell to the Swallows* (1853) and *Pen and Pencil Pictures* (1854), before becoming editor of the *Liskeard Gazette* in 1858. Over the course of the rest of his life, Hood produced a wide variety of work, from poetry (*Daughters of King Daher, and other Poems*, 1861) to children's fiction (*Jingles and Jokes for the Little Folks*, 1865) and adult novels (*Captain Masters's Children*, 1865). He was also an accomplished short story writer and illustrator. From 1865 onwards he edited the weekly *Punch*-esque magazine *Fun,* which became popular under his direction. Hood died in 1874, aged just 39.

A Brief History of Poetry

'Poetry' as an art form, has an incredibly long history – it may even predate literacy and the written word. At its purest, poetry is simply a form of communication using aesthetic and rhythmic qualities of language to evoke meanings over and above the ostensible and everyday meaning of words. The earliest poetry is believed to have been recited or sung; employed as a way of remembering oral history, genealogy, and law.

Many scholars, particularly those researching the Homeric tradition and the oral epics of the Balkans, suggest that early writing shows clear traces of older oral traditions, including the use of repeated phrases as building blocks in larger poetic units. A rhythmic and repetitious form would make a long story easier to remember and retell, before writing was available as an *aide-memoire*. Thus many ancient works, from the Vedas (1700 - 1200 BCE) to the *Odyssey* (800 - 675 BCE), appear to have been composed in poetic form to aid memorization and oral transmission. Poetry appears among the earliest records of most literate cultures, with poetic fragments found on early monoliths, runestones and stelae.

The oldest surviving speculative fiction poem is the *Tale of the Shipwrecked Sailor*, written in *Hieratic* and ascribed a date around 2500 BCE. Other sources ascribe the earliest written poetry to the *Epic of Gilgamesh* written in *cuneiform*; however, it is most likely that *The Tale of the Shipwrecked Sailor* predates *Gilgamesh* by half a millennium. The oldest epic poetry besides the *Epic of Gilgamesh* are the Greek epics *Iliad* and *Odyssey*, and the Indian Sanskrit epics *Ramayana and Mahabharata*.

In the Western poetic tradition, meters are customarily grouped according to a characteristic 'metrical foot' and the number of feet per line. The number of metrical feet in a line are described using Greek terminology: tetrameter for four feet and hexameter for six feet, for example. Thus, 'iambic pentameter' is a meter comprising five feet per line, in which the predominant kind of foot is the 'iamb'. This metric system originated in ancient Greek poetry, and was used by poets such as Pindar and Sappho, and by the great tragedians of Athens. Similarly, 'dactylic hexameter', comprises six feet per line, of which the dominant kind of foot is the 'dactyl'. Dactylic hexameter was the traditional meter of Greek epic poetry, the earliest extant examples of which are the works of Homer and Hesiod. Iambic pentameter and dactylic hexameter were later used by a number of poets, including William Shakespeare and Henry Wadsworth Longfellow.

Different traditions and genres of poetry tend to use different meters, ranging from the Shakespearean iambic pentameter and the Homeric dactylic hexameter to the anapestic tetrameter used in many nursery rhymes. Rhyme, alliteration, assonance and consonance are ways of creating repetitive patterns of sound. They may be used as an independent structural element in a poem, to reinforce rhythmic patterns, or as an ornamental element. They can also carry a meaning separate from the repetitive sound patterns created. For example, Chaucer used heavy alliteration to mock Old English verse and to paint a character as archaic. Poetry can also rely on a heavy visual aspect, often underappreciated. Even before the advent of printing, the visual appearance of poetry often added meaning or depth. In Arabic, Hebrew, Chinese, and much modernist poetry, the visual presentation of finely calligraphed poems has played an important part in the overall effect.

Ancient thinkers sought to determine what makes poetry distinctive as a form and what distinguishes good poetry from bad, resulting in the development of 'poetics', or the study of the aesthetics of poetry. Some ancient societies, such as the Chinese through the *Classic of History*, one of the 'Five Classics', developed canons of poetic works that had ritual as well as aesthetic importance. More recently, thinkers have struggled to find a definition that could encompass formal differences as great as those between Chaucer's *The Canterbury Tales* and Matsuo Bashō's *Oku no Hosomichi*, as well as differences in context that span from the religious poetry of the Tanakh, to love poetry, to rap.

Classical thinkers employed classification as a way to define and assess the quality of poetry. Notably, the existing fragments of Aristotle's *Poetics* describe three genres of poetry – the epic, the comic, and the tragic – and develop rules to distinguish the highest-quality poetry in each genre, based on the underlying purposes of the genre. Aristotle's work was influential throughout the Middle East during the Islamic Golden Age, as well as in Europe during the Renaissance. Later poets and aestheticians often distinguished poetry from, and defined it in opposition to prose, which was generally understood as writing with a proclivity to logical explication and a linear narrative structure.

This does not imply that poetry is illogical or lacks narration, but rather that poetry is an attempt to render the beautiful or sublime without the burden of engaging the logical or narrative thought process. English Romantic poet John Keats termed this escape from logic 'Negative Capability'. This 'romantic' approach views form as a key element of successful poetry because form is abstract and distinct from the underlying notional logic. This approach remained influential into the twentieth century. During this period, there was also substantially more interaction among the various poetic traditions, in part due to the spread of European colonialism and the attendant rise in global trade. In addition to this, there was a boom in translation during the Romantic period, when numerous ancient works were rediscovered.

The rejection of traditional forms and structures for poetry that began in the first half of the twentieth century coincided with a questioning of the purpose and meaning of traditional definitions of poetry – and of distinctions between poetry and prose, particularly given examples of poetic prose and prosaic poetry. Numerous modernist poets have written in non-traditional forms or in what traditionally would have been considered prose, although their writing was generally infused with poetic diction and often with rhythm and tone established by non-metrical means. Recently, postmodernism has come to convey more completely prose and poetry as distinct entities, and also among genres of poetry, as having meaning only as cultural artefacts. Postmodernism goes beyond modernism's emphasis on the creative role of the poet, to emphasize the role of the reader of a text (Hermeneutics), and to highlight the complex cultural web within which a poem is read.

Today, throughout the world, poetry often incorporates poetic form and diction from other cultures and from the past, further confounding attempts at definition and classification that were once sensible within a tradition such as the Western canon. There are an astounding array of 'types' of poetry, for instance historical epics, poetry for liturgical purposes (hymns, psalms, suras and hadiths), popular music, elegies, romance and tragedies, political invective, and light hearted nursery or nonsense rhymes. The use of verse to transmit cultural information continues in the present, and the poetic arts show no signs of abating – in fact, their development continues apace. It is hoped that the current reader enjoys this book on the subject.

NOTE

BY THE AMERICAN EDITOR.

IT is now ten or a dozen years since there appeared in London a little volume called "The Rules of Rhyme," and signed by Tom Hood. The author of this manual of versification was the only son of the Thomas Hood who sang the "Song of the Shirt" and wrote "Whims and Oddities," who mingled smiles and tears all his life long, making a brave fight against disease and death, until at last the latter won the victory, snatching him from the bed whereon he lay "spitting blood and puns." Named after his father, Thomas Hood the younger took to his father's trade, and led the laborious life of a working journalist all his days. Proud of his father's name, he chose always to sign himself "Tom Hood," that he might not be accused of trying to trade on his father's reputation. He was born in 1835, and he died toward the end of 1874. He began life as a clerk in the War Office, a position he gave up in 1865, when he became editor of "Fun." In the course of his literary career he wrote four or five novels, of which at least one—"For Valor"—was republished in this country; and he edited as many Christmas annuals. In 1868 he published his first "Comic Annual," in imitation of his father, and so popular did he make it that it continues to appear even now, seven years after his death. He also wrote and illustrated many books for children. As editor of "Fun," he showed that he was also the author of "Rules of Rhyme"; he practiced what he preached, and he neither wrote nor tolerated slipshod rhyme and halting rhythm. While he edited "Fun," its verse—comic or serious, pathetic or satiric—had always a high degree of technical merit. He could not make poets of all those who wrote verse for the paper; but he could and did make them mend their paces and mind their stops. He was only a minor poet himself, but he had a keen understanding of verse and great metrical facility, as any one may see who considers the posthumous volume of his poems edited by his sister, Frances Freeling Broderip.

In the present edition the American editor has dealt very freely with the English author's text, treating Tom Hood's "Rules of Rhyme" very much as he treated the "Young Poet's Guide" when he reprinted it as a supplement to his own treatise. He has made occasional alterations, a few omissions, and more frequent insertions. The most of the added matter is indicated by brackets, [thus]. It has been deemed inadvisable to point out in detail all the minor changes, and it is hoped that a general acknowledgment here will suffice. Three whole chapters have been added—one on the sonnet, another on the *rondeau* and the *ballade*, and a third on the other fixed forms of verse. The brief dictionary of rhymes has been revised, simplified, rearranged, and somewhat enlarged; and to it have been prefixed a few lines of Ben Jonson's on the difficulties and dangers of rhyme, which seemed pertinent. A. P.

CONTENTS.

	PAGE
NOTE BY THE AMERICAN EDITOR	3
INTRODUCTION (BY TOM HOOD)	9
CHAP. I.—VERSE GENERALLY	17
II.—CLASSIC VERSIFICATION	25
III.—GUIDES AND HAND-BOOKS	34
IV.—OF FEET AND CÆSURA	42
V.—METER AND RHYTHM	46
VI.—OF RHYME	65
VII.—OF FIGURES	71
VIII.—OF BURLESQUE AND COMIC VERSE, AND *VERS DE SOCIÉTÉ*	76
IX.—OF SONG-WRITING	83
X.—OF THE SONNET	86
XI.—OF THE RONDEAU AND THE *BALLADE*	91
XII.—OF OTHER FIXED FORMS OF VERSE	105
A FIT OF RHYME AGAINST RHYME (BY BEN JONSON)	119
A DICTIONARY OF RHYMES	123

INTRODUCTION.

I AM anxious at the first outset that the object of this work should not be misunderstood. It does not assume to be a hand-book for poets, or a guide to poetry. The attempt to compile such a book as is implied by either of those titles would be as absurd as pretentious.

A poet, to paraphrase the Latin, is created, not manufactured. Cicero's "nascimur poetæ, fimus oratores,"* is, with some modification, even more to the point. In a word, poetical genius is a gift, but education and perseverance will make almost any man a versifier.

All, therefore, that this book aims to teach is the art of versification. That art, like logic, is "ars instrumentalis, dirigens mentem inter

---

* "We are born poets; we make ourselves orators."

cognitionem rerum."* As logic does not supply you with arguments, but only defines the mode in which they are to be expressed or used, so versification does not teach you how to write poetry, but how to construct verse. It may be a means to the end, but it does not pretend to assure its attainment. Versification and logic are to poetry and reason what a parapet is to a bridge: they do not convey you across, but prevent you from falling over. The difference is that which exists between τέχνη and ἐπιστήμη.†

This definition is rendered necessary by the Dogberry spirit which is now abroad, and which insists that "to be a well-favored man is the gift of fortune"—fortune in the sense of wealth, I presume—"but to write and read comes by nature"; in fact, that, to be "a poet," a man needs to be advantageously placed in the world, but that any one can "write poetry."

---

* "An instrumental art, directing the mind to the knowledge of things."

† "Art" and "science."

With this conviction, I have discarded the title of a guide for "poets," feeling that there is much real poetry that is not in verse, and a vast deal of verse that is not poetry; and that, therefore, "a hard and fast line" was of the first importance to mark the boundary of my undertaking. Poetry is far less a question of manner than of matter, whereas versification is purely a question of form. I will even venture to say that some of our noblest poems are in prose; and that many great poets have been but inferior versifiers. But what these last wrote has possessed qualities compared with which the mere mechanism of their verse is as nothing. The poet gives to the world in his sublime thoughts diamonds of the purest water. It would be idle to quibble about minor points of the polishing and setting of such gems—they would lose in the process! But the writer of verse does not—and should not—pretend to give us diamonds. He offers paste brilliants; and therefore it the more behooves him to see to the perfection of the cutting, on which their beauty depends.

The thoughts presented by the poet may be rough-hewn; the fancies of the versifier must be accurately finished, and becomingly set. Poetry, therefore, abounds in licenses, while versification boasts only of laws.

To enumerate, explain, and define these laws is the object of this work. Nor is such a task a waste of time, as those may be inclined to think who argue that, if one can not write poetry, 'tis absurd to try to write verse. Yet versification is an elegant accomplishment, to say the least—" emollit mores, nec sinit esse feros."* But it is something more than an elegant accomplishment—much more.

In the dead languages—leaving in abeyance the question of classical *versus* mathematical education—nothing gives such scholarly finish as the practice of Greek and Latin verse-writing, nothing such an intimate knowledge and understanding of the genius of either language.

Were English versification taught in our schools, I believe the boys would acquire a

---

* " It softens the manners and forbids their roughness."

better understanding and appreciation of their own tongue. With such training, a lad would shrink from a mispronunciation as he does from a false quantity in Latin or Greek. He would not fall into the slipshod way of pronouncing "doing" as if it were spelled "doin'," and "written and spoken" as if "writtun and spokun." He would not make dissyllables of words like "fire" and "mire," or of the trisyllable "really." Nor would he make another mistake (very common now, as revealed in magazine verse where such words are put to rhyme, "before" and "more") of pronouncing "ure" as "ore"—"shore" and "asshore" for "sure" and "assure," of which, of course, the correct pronunciation is "shewre," "ashewre."*

The purging of our pronunciation would be of general benefit. At present it is shifting and uncertain, because it is never taught. Surely the deterioration of our language is not

---

* The derivation of this vulgarism is ancient, and not very dignified. "Sewer" and "shore," meaning a drain, are, of course, the same word. It seems absurd, when we have so few vowels, to allow the distinctive sound of any of them to be lost, as it would be in this case, by the "o" and "u" becoming interchanged.—(T. H.)

a minor matter, and when it can be removed by the encouragement of verse-writing at our schools, strictly and clearly taught, it seems astonishing that no effort has been made in that direction.*

However, whether, by establishing a system of English versifying at our schools, we shall ever endeavor to give fixity to our pronunciation, is a question hardly likely, I fear, to be brought to the test yet awhile. That English versifying is a strong educational power, I do not doubt, and, in that belief, have endeavored to render this hand-book as complete as possible. I have therefore laid down the most stringent rules and the clearest formulæ in my power.

Verse is but the A B C of poetry, and the student must learn his alphabet correctly. We should not allow a child to arrange the letters as he chose—" A, Z, B, G, C "—nor must the

---

* There is one decided advantage to the public which would accrue from the teaching of versification in schools. We should be saved the infliction of much nonsense, published under the name of poetry. For it is to be hoped that no man, who had been well-grounded in the mechanism of verse as a lad, would think of publishing in mature age what he would know were but school-exercises only, and not poems.—(T. H.)

beginner in verse dream of using any licenses of a similar kind. I should fail in my duty if I admitted anything of the kind; for, while it would be presumption to lay down laws for poets, it would be incapacity to frame licenses for versifiers.

I therefore conclude these prefatory remarks by adducing the two chief regulations for the student:

> First. That he must use such rhymes only as are perfect to the ear, when correctly pronounced.
>
> Second. That he must never write a line which will not sooner or later in the stanza have a line to correspond with a rhyme.

To these I may add, as a rider, this piece of advice (somewhat in the style of the whist maxim, "When in doubt, play a trump"): If you have reason to choose between two styles of versification, select the more difficult.

It is only by sustaining your verse at the highest elevation that you can hope even to approach poetry.

"Be bold—be bold—but not too bold!"

And bear in mind the words of Sir Philip Sidney: "Who shootes at the midday Sonne, though he be sure he shall neuer hit the marke; yet as sure he is, he shall shoote higher than who aymes but at a bush."

T. H.

CHAPTER I.

VERSE GENERALLY.

THERE is no better text for this chapter than some
lines from Pope's " Essay on Criticism ":

" But most by numbers judge a poet's song,
And smooth or rough, with them, is right or wrong:
These equal syllables alone require,
Tho' oft the ear the open vowels tire ;
5 While expletives their feeble aid do join ;
And ten low words oft creep in one dull line :
While they ring round the same unvaried chimes,
With sure returns of still recurring rhymes ;
Where'er you find ' the cooling western breeze,'
10 In the next line it 'whispers through the trees':
If crystal streams ' with pleasing murmurs creep,'
The reader's threaten'd—not in vain—with 'sleep.'
Then at the last and only couplet, fraught
With some unmeaning thing they call a thought,
15 A needless Alexandrine ends the song,
That, like a wounded snake, drags its slow length along.
Leave such to tune their own dull rhymes, to know
What's roundly smooth, or languishingly slow ;
And praise the easy vigor of a line
20 Where Denham's strength and Waller's sweetness join.

True ease in writing comes from art, not chance,
As those move easiest who have learned to dance.
'Tis not enough no harshness gives offence,
The sound must seem an echo to the sense.
25 Soft is the strain when zephyr gently blows,
And the smooth stream in smoother numbers flows;
But when loud surges lash the sounding shore,
The hoarse rough verse should like the torrent roar;
When Ajax strives some rock's vast weight to throw,
30 The line, too, labors, and the words move slow.
Not so, when swift Camilla scours the plain,
Flies o'er th' unbending corn, and skims along the main."

Johnson sneers somewhat at the attempt at what he styles "representative meter." He quotes "one of the most successful attempts"—

" With many a weary step, and many a groan,
Up a high hill he heaves a huge round stone;
The huge round stone, resulting with a bound,
Thunders impetuous down and smokes along the ground."

After admitting that he sees the stone move slowly upward, and roll violently back, he says, "try the same numbers to another sense—

" While many a merry tale and many a song
Cheer'd the rough road, we wish'd the rough road long.
The rough road then returning in a round
Mock'd our impatient steps, for all was fairy ground."

"We have now," says the Doctor, "lost much of the delay and much of the rapidity." Truly so!— but why? The choice of words has really altered the measure, though not the number of syllables. If we look at the second line of the first extract, we see how the frequent use of the aspirate, with a long sound after it, gives the labor of the ascent. There is nothing of this in the corresponding line, where the "r" gives a run rather than a halt to the measure. But Johnson more decidedly shows how he was mistaken when he finds fault with Pope's—

> " The varying verse, the full resounding line,
>   The long majestic march, and energy divine."

His objection to this is, that the same sequence of syllables gives "the rapid race" and "the march of slow-paced majesty"; and he adds, "the exact prosodist will find the line of *swiftness* by one time longer than that of *tardiness*." By this it is to be presumed he alludes to the trisyllabic nature of the first foot of the first line—"varying." But it is just that which gives the rapidity. The other half of the line is not meant to give rapidity, but "resounding." The second line, by the repetition of the "a" in "march" and "majesty," gives the tramp of the march to admiration.

So much for Johnson's objections. We will now see how far the lines of Pope can guide us in the construction of verse.

LINE THIRD indicates the necessity—which Pope himself, even, did not adequately recognize—the necessity of varying the fall of the verse on the ear. Pope did this by graduating his accents. The line should scan with an accented syllable following an unaccented one—

"And smooth' or rough', with them', is right' or wrong'."
Pope varied this by a sort of compromise—

"And the' smooth stream' in smoother' numbers' flows',"
would be the right scansion. But the accent passes in a subdued form from "the" to "smooth," which pleasantly modulates the line, and gives the flow required for the figure treated of.*

But there was another means of varying the verse which was not in those days adopted. It was not then recognized that there were some cases in which the unaccented syllable might have two "beats." Pope wrote,

"The gen'rous pleasure to be charm'd with wit."

Had he written "generous," it might have stood, and would have given a variety. And this would have saved the eyesore of such lines as—

"T' admire superior sense and doubt our own."

LINE FOURTH does not exactly describe the fault it commits. "The open vowel" is no offense, but rather a beauty, though like all beauty it must not be too lavishly displayed. The fault of the line really lies in the repetition of the same broad sound—"o." The

---

* An instance of the contrary effect will be found in Tennyson's line—

"Long lines of cliff breaking had left a chasm."

Here the proper stress should be "break'ing," according to scansion, but the accent thrown back on the first syllable gives a sudden sort of halt suggestive of the fall of the cliff.—(T. H.)

same vowel-sounds should not be repeated in a line.* This especially holds good where they are so associated with consonants as to form a rhyme, or anything approaching to it.

LINE FIFTH points out an inelegance which no one with any ear could be guilty of—the use of " do " and " did," to eke out a line or help a rhyme.

LINE SIXTH indicates a practice which those who have studied Latin versification would avoid without such a hint, since the nature of the cæsura compels the avoidance of monosyllables.

LINE NINTH, with the following three lines, warns against an error which naturally becomes the more frequent the longer English verse is written, since rhymes become more and more hackneyed every day.

LINE SIXTEENTH. The Alexandrine will come under discussion in its place among meters.

LINE TWENTY-FIRST might well serve for a motto for this little treatise. If a poet said this of poetry, how much more does it apply to versification!

LINE TWENTY-FIFTH. Here, and in the following line, by delicate manipulation of the accent, Pope gets the desired effect. Instead of "So soft' the strain'," he attracts the ear with "Soft' is," and the unexpected word gives the key-note of the line.

LINE TWENTY-SEVENTH. It is almost needless

---

* Yet this is not all that is requisite to make music. Browning, I think I may say, never repeats the same sound; Tennyson frequently does; yet the latter's verse has a better flow than the former's. But this may be the result of other arts employed by the Laureate.—(T. H.)

to point out how in this, and the next line, the poet, by artful management of accent and careful selection of onomatopoetic words, gives the required assonance to the lines.

LINE TWENTY-NINTH. The broad vowels here give the requisite pause and "deliberation" to the verse. In the following line, the introduction of "too" —(under some circumstances it might well come under the condemnation of Line Fifth)—makes the line labor, and the open "o" at the end of the line "tires the ear."

LINE THIRTY-FIRST. Here the poet gets the slide of the "s" to give the idea of motion. In the following line, by the elision and the apt introduction of short syllables, he repeats the notion. In my opinion the artistic skill of Pope is peculiarly observable in the last few couplets. In the first line in each instance the effect is produced by the use of a different artifice from that employed in the second.

These rules were of course intended by Pope to apply only to the measure called "heroic," i. e., decasyllabic verse. But, *mutatis mutandis*, they will be equally applicable to general verse.

Coleridge, in his "Christabel," struck out what he considered a new meter, which he describes as "not, properly speaking, irregular, though it may seem so from its being founded on a new principle: namely, that of counting in each line the accents, not the syllables. Though the latter may vary from seven to twelve, yet in each line the accents will be found to be only four." This was a decided step in the right direction, being in truth a recognition of the principle that measure in English was not exhausted—was, indeed, hardly satisfied—by the old rule of thumb; that, in short, it needed a compromise between *accent* and *quantity*.

Southey, in his "Thalaba," essayed a new style of versification, of which he writes as follows:

"It were easy to make a parade of learning by enumerating the various feet which it admits; it is only needful to observe that no two lines are employed in sequence which can be read into one. Two six-syllable lines (it will perhaps be answered) compose an Alexandrine; the truth is, that the Alexandrine, when harmonious, is composed of two six-syllable lines. One advantage this meter assuredly possesses; the dullest reader can not distort it into discord. . . . I do not wish the *improvisatore* time, but something that denotes the sense of harmony; something like the accent of feeling; like the tone which every poet necessarily gives to poetry." Of course, by "six syllables" Southey means "six feet." He was evidently struggling for emancipation from the old rule of thumb.

[After Southey and Coleridge came Edgar Allen Poe, who went a step further, and in his essay on the "Rationale of Verse" pointed out the path of true progress and indicated the only way in which we could hope to get light on the meters and rhythms of the past. Poe's essay should be attentively studied by all who wish to understand the mechanism of verse.]

Of late many eccentricities of versification have been attempted after the manner of Mr. Whitman, but for these, like the Biblical echo of Mr. Tupper's muse, there seem to be no perceptible rules, even should it be desirable to imitate them.

I would here add a few words of advice to those who, by the study of our greatest writers, would endeavor to improve their own style. For smoothness I should say Waller, in preference even to Pope, because the former wrote in far more various measures, and may challenge comparison with Pope, on Pope's own ground, with "The Ode to the Lord Protector," in decasyllabic verse. For music—"lilt" is an expressive word that exactly conveys what I mean—they can not do better than choose Herrick. Add to these two George Herbert, and I think the student will have a valuable guide in small space. [Add, also, Longfellow, who is a master of meters and whose verse has a singing simplicity equaled only by Heine's—if by his.]

CHAPTER II.

CLASSIC VERSIFICATION.

IT was once thought that the best and easiest way of learning English grammar was through the Latin. That English versification can not be similarly acquired through the Latin is due to the fact that the Latin system depends on quantity, and the English chiefly on accent and rhyme. Nevertheless, a slight acquaintance with the classic measures will prove useful to the student of English verse. In the absence of all teaching of English versification at our schools, they have done good service in giving our boys some insight into the structure of verse.

The structure of Latin and Greek verse depends on the quantity—the length or shortness expressed by the forms $-\smile$. A long syllable is equal in duration to two short syllables, which may therefore take its place (as it may take theirs) in certain positions. The combinations of syllables are called feet, of which there are about nine-and-twenty. Seven of the most common are here given:

Spondee $--$	Iambus $\smile -$	Anapæst $\smile\smile -$
Trochee $-\smile$	Dactyl $-\smile\smile$	Amphimacer $-\smile -$
	Amphibrach $\smile-\smile$	

[In a " Lesson for a Boy," written for his son Derwent, Coleridge has described and exemplified these feet in English :

" Trochee trips from long to short ;
  From long to long in solemn sort
  Slow Spondee stalks ; strong foot ! yet ill able
  Ever to come up with Dactyl trisyllable ;
  Iambics march from short to long ;
  With a leap and a bound the swift Anapests throng ;
  One syllable long, with a short at each side,
  Amphibrachy hastes with a stately stride ;
  First and last being long, middle short, Amphimacer
    Strikes his thundering hoofs, like a proud high-bred racer."]

Of the styles of verse produced by combinations of these feet the most important are the Heroic, or Hexameter ; the Elegiac, alternate Hexameters and Pentameters ; and the Dramatic or Iambic. All others may be classed as Lyrics.

The Cæsura (division) is the separation of each verse into two parts by the ending of a word in the middle of a certain foot.* It may be here noted that this principle (the ending of a word in the middle of a foot) applies generally to the verse, it being an inelegance to construct lines of words of which each constitutes a foot. The well-known line of Virgil, marked to show the feet, will explain this at a glance—

" Arma vi|rumque ca|no || Tro|jæ qui | primus ab | oris."

---

* The cæsura in some cases falls at the end of the foot.—(T. H.)

CLASSIC VERSIFICATION. 27

In this the cæsura occurs in the third foot, between *cano* and *Trojæ*. But in no case is one foot composed of one word only.

The Hexameter line consists of, practically, five dactyls and a spondee or trochee. A spondee may take the place of each of the first four dactyls—and sometimes, but very rarely, of the fifth. The cæsura falls in the third foot at the end of the first—and sometimes at the end of the second—syllable of the dactyl. In some cases it is in the fourth foot, after the first syllable. The last word in the line should be either a dissyllable or trisyllable.

The Pentameter is never used alone, but, with an Hexameter preceding it in the distich, forms Elegiac Verse. It consists of two parts, divided by a cæsura, each part composed of two dactyls (interchangeable with spondees) and a long syllable.* The last place in the line should be occupied by a dissyllabic word—at least it should not be a monosyllable or trisyllable.

The Iambic is most commonly used in a six-foot line of iambics (the trimeter iambic; see the note on last paragraph). In the first, third, and fifth place a spondee may be substituted, and there are other licenses which we need not here enter upon, as the measure is not of much importance for our purposes. The cæsura occurs in the third or fourth foot.

---

* The name Pentameter (*five*-foot) is derived from the long syllables being incomplete feet, and counting together as one, so as to make five with the four dactyls. In anapæstics and iambics the *meter* is a dipod, i. e., it includes two feet, so that an iambic dimeter contains not two but four iambics.—(T. H.)

The Lyrics are, as a rule, compound verses; different sorts of feet enter into the formation of the lines; and the stanzas consist of lines of different kinds, and are styled strophes.

The chief of the lyric measures are the Sapphic and Alcaic.

The Sapphic is a combination of three Sapphic verses with an Adonic.

Lines 1, 2, 3, $-\smile\,|\,-\,-\,|\,-\,||\smile\smile\,|\,-\smile\,|\,-\asymp$
Line 4, $-\smile\smile\,|\,-\,-$

The double line represents the cæsura, which in rare instances falls a syllable later.

The Alcaic is, like the Sapphic, a four-line stanza. Its scheme is:

Lines 1 and 2, $\asymp -\,|\smile -\,|\,-\,||\,-\smile\smile\,|\,-\smile\asymp$
Line 3, $\asymp -\,|\smile -\,|\,-\,-\,|\smile -\,|\asymp$
Line 4, $-\smile\smile\,|\,-\smile\smile\,|\,-\smile\,|\,-\asymp$

That is to say, it consists of two eleven-syllable, one nine-syllable, and one ten-syllable Alcaic lines (Alcaici hendeka-, ennea-, and deka-syllabici). Much of the success of the stanza depends on the flow of the third line, which, according to the best models, should consist of three trisyllables (or equivalent combinations, e. g., a dissyllable noun with its monosyllabic preposition).

When it is stated that Horace wrote in four- or five-and-twenty lyric measures, it will be obvious that I can not exhaust, or attempt to exhaust, the list of measures in a work like this. The reader will have acquired some notion of the nature of classic versification, from what I have stated of Latin composition applying with unimportant differences to Greek. Those who have the leisure or the inclination might do worse than study Greek and Latin poetry, if only to see if they can suggest no novelties of meter. I can recall no English verse that reproduces Horace's musical measure:

"Mĭsĕrār' est | nĭqu' ămōrĭ dărĕ lūdŭm | nĕqŭe dŭlcī
Mălă vīnŏ—lăvĕr' aut ĕx|ănĭmārī | mĕtŭēntēs
Pătrŭæ vĕr|bĕră linguæ."

[Poe rebelled against accepted principles of classic prosody. In his essay on the "Rationale of Verse" he declared that "employing from among the numerous *ancient* feet the spondee, the trochee, the iambus, the anapæst, the dactyl, and the cæsura alone," he engaged "to scan correctly any of the Horatian rhythms, or any true rhythm that human ingenuity can conceive." He denounces all the classic feet save those just named, and even denies their existence "except in the brains of the scholiasts.]

Greek verse seems a less promising field than Latin at a first glance. But one of the choruses in Aristophanes's " Plutus " has an exact echo in English verse·

" ἄνδρες φίλοι καὶ δημόται καὶ τοῦ πονεῖν ἐρασταί,"

may fairly run in a curricle with

"A captain bold of Halifax who lived in country quarters."

The great difficulty of finding a corresponding measure in English for Latin or Greek verse, on the accepted theory that the English acute accent answers to the Latin long quantity, and the grave accent to the short, will be found in the spondee. We have no means of replacing the two longs in juxtaposition, and are compelled to find refuge in what, according to the accent-quantity theory, is either an iamb or a trochee.

I subjoin the following attempts to render a few Latin meters, commencing with a translation of the Horatian measure just alluded to:

"Hapless lasses who in glasses may not drown those pangs of passion,
Or disclose its bitter woes, it's—so they tell you—not the fashion."

Yet this, in spite of the sub-rhymes which give the swing of the Ionicus (⌣ ⌣ -′-) may well be read as a succession of trochees—that is to say, according to the quantity-accent system.

Here is an attempt at the Sapphic:

"Never—ah me—now, as in days aforetime
Rises o'erwhelming memory—'t is banish'd!
Scenes of loved childhood, can not ye restore time,
Though it has vanish'd?"

The Alcaic measure is essayed in the following:

"Ah woe! the men who gallantly sallying
Strode forth undaunted, rapidly rallying—
No longer advancing attack-ward,
Rush'd a disorderly tumult backward."

In these, again, the difficulty of exactly replacing quantity by accident is great—if not insurmountable. Hence it is that, as a rule, the attempts at giving the exact reproductions of Latin measures have failed. Nevertheless, I believe that corresponding measures, suitable to the genius of our language, may be suggested by a study of the classics.

The often-quoted lines of Coleridge on the hexameter and pentameter appear to me faulty :

"In the hex|ameter | rises | the | fountain's | silvery | column—
In the pen|tameter | aye | falling in | melody | back."

The first feet of both lines are less dactyls than anapæsts. The cæsura of the first line is not the "worthier" cæsura. In the second line the monosyllable is inadmissible in the last place. [Better are the lines of Coleridge in which the Homeric hexameter is described and exemplified :

"Strongly it bears us along in swelling and limitless billows—
Nothing before and nothing behind but the sky and the ocean."]

Here I may as well point out what seems to me to be a difficulty of English versification which has given much trouble. The substitution of accent for quantity is not all that is required to make the best verse. Quantity enters into the consideration too. A combination of consonants, giving an almost imperceptible weight to the vowel preceding them, goes far to disqualify it for a place as an unaccented syllable. To my thinking "rises a" would be a better English dactyl than "rises the," and "falls it in" than "falling in." But no agglomeration of consonants can make such a syllable accented. Two lines from Coleridge's "Mahomet" will evidence this :

"Huge wasteful | empires | founded and | hallowed | slow perse|cution,
  Soul-wither|ing but | crush'd the | blasphemous | rites of the | Pagan."

"Huge wasteful" is not a dactyl, and "ing but" is certainly not a spondee—nor is "crushed the." "Hallowed," by force of the broad "o," is almost perfect as a spondee, on the other hand; as is "empires" also. Longfellow, in his "Evangeline," has, perhaps, done the best that can be done to give an exact rendering of the Latin hexameter; but Tennyson, in portions of "Maud," has caught its spirit, and transfused it into an English form. No poet, indeed, has done so much as the Laureate to introduce new or revive old forms of versification, and enrich the language with musical measure.

It may be well to note here that the classic poets did not forget the use of the maxim which Pope expresses in the line—

"The sound must seem an echo to the sense."

In this they were greatly assisted by the use of the quantity, which enabled them the more readily to give rapidity or weight to their lines. Nothing could more admirably represent a horse's gallop than the beat of the words—

"Quadrupedante putrem sonitu quatit ungula campum."

The unwieldiness of the Cyclops is splendidly shadowed in the line—

"Monstrum, horrendum, informe, ingens cui lumen ademptum."

CLASSIC VERSIFICATION.

And again the beat of the Cyclopean hammers is well imitated in the verse—

"Illi inter sese magnâ vi brachia tollunt."

Too much stress may easily be laid on this adornment, and some poets have carried it to excess. But the beginner in verse will do well not to overlook it.

NOTE.—The Poet Laureate, whose mastery of meter is remarkable, has given us alcaics in his lines to Milton—

"Oh, mighty-mouth'd inventor of harmonies,
Oh, skill'd to sing of time and eternity,
God-gifted organ-voice of England—
Milton, a name to resound for ages."

I would especially commend to those whom these remarks have interested in any way the perusal, with a view to this particular object, of "Father Prout's Reliques."—(T. H.)

CHAPTER III.

GUIDES AND HAND-BOOKS.

THE earliest hand-book of verse appears to be that of Bysshe, who is, by the way, described in the British Museum Catalogue as "the Poet." The entry is the only ground I can find for so describing him. He is, however, amusingly hard on simple versifiers: "Such Debasers of Rhyme, and Dablers in Poetry would do well to consider that a Man would justly deserve a higher Esteem in the World by being a good Mason or Shoe-Maker, than by being an indifferent or second-Rate Poet." Furthermore, with touching modesty, he says, "I pretend not by the following sheets to teach a man to be a Poet in Spight of Fate and Nature."

His dictionary of rhymes is better than those of his successors—perhaps I should say "that" of his successors, for Walker's has been repeated with all its errors, or nearly all, in every subsequent hand-book. Bysshe is to be praised for setting his face against what Walker styles "allowable" rhymes, such as "haste" and "feast." He, however, seems to have been curiously ignorant of the ever-changing nature of English pronunciation. When Pope rhymed "line" and "join," and "obey" and "tea," it was the fashion to pronounce "join" as "jine" and "tea" as "tay."

Bysshe's theory of verse was "the seat of the accent, and the pause," as distinguished from quantity—that is, it depended on the number of syllables. As a result of this undivided devotion, he misses much of the power to be attained by making the sound the echo of the sense, as Pope puts it. He proposes to alter a line of Dryden's from

"But forced, harsh, and uneasy unto all,"
into
"But forced and harsh, uneasy unto all."

One would fancy the merest tyro would see the intentional harshness of the line as Dryden wrote it, and its utter emasculation as Bysshe re-forms it.

Bysshe is strongly in favor of clipping syllables, a very pitiable error, for the chief drawback of English as a poetical language is the preponderance of consonants. He prefers to make "beauteous" dissyllabic and "victorious" trisyllabic. He recommends the elision which makes "bower," "Heaven," "Prayer," and "higher," monosyllables, and advises the use of such abortions as "temp'rance," "fab'lous," "med'cine," "cov'nant," and even "wall'wing" for wallowing! To compensate for these clippings, however, he considers "ism" a dissyllable!

As a consequence of his narrowing verse to a question of syllable and accent only, he vulgarizes many words unnecessarily. The student of verse who considers quantity as well as accent will find no difficulty in reading the following lines without eliding any vowels :

"From diamond quarries hewn, and rocks of gold."—*Milton.*

"A violet by a mossy stone."—*Wordsworth.*

"With vain but violent force their darts they threw."—*Cowley.*

"His ephod, mitre, well-cut diadem on."—*Cowley.*

"My blushing hyacinth and my bays I keep."—*Dryden.*

Bysshe cuts down to "di'mond," "vi'let," "vi'lent," "di'dem," "hy'cinth," words which need no such debasing elision. As in music two short sharp beats are equivalent to one long one (two minims = one semibreve), so in verse two brief vowels, or syllables even, are admissible—indeed, at times desirable for the sake of variety in lieu of one.

Among less questionable maxims of Bysshe's is one, "avoid a concourse of vowels," instanced by—

"Sould thy *I*ambics swell into a book."

This means, it is to be presumed, "avoid a concourse of repetitions of one sound," a very necessary rule. Some poets are careful not to get the same vowel sound twice in any line. "Avoid ending a verse with an adjective whose substantive follows in the next line" is another sound precept, instanced by—

"Some lost their quiet rivals, some their kind Parents."

The same rule applies to the separation of a preposition from the case which it governs, as exemplified in—

"The daily lessening of our life shows by
A little dying," etc.

With less reason Bysshe condemns alliteration. It is an artifice that can be overdone, as is often the case in Poe's poems, and those of Mr. Swinburne. Alliteration is a means, not an end. So long as alliterative verse pleases the ear, and yet does not betray to its reader the cause of the pleasant sensation, it is an admirable addition to the beauty of the verse. But as soon as it attracts the reader's attention, as a *tour de force*, it is a blot, because it inflicts an injury on the poem by engaging the mind on the machinery instead of the matter. Instead of thinking how exquisite the poem is, we are wondering how often that clever contortionist, the poet, will fling his somersault of alliteration.

Following the example of the old "Gradus ad Parnassum," Bysshe gives an anthology with his guide. An anthology in a guide to English verse is worse than useless, for it serves no purpose save to provoke plagiarism and imitation. Any one who wishes to write verse will do little unless he has a fair acquaintance with English poetry—an acquaintance for which an anthology can never be a substitute; while it will but cripple and hamper his fancy and originality by supplying him with quotations on any given subject, from "April" to "Woman."

Walker's "Rhyming Dictionary" has greater faults,

but also greater merits, than Bysshe's "Art of Poetry." Walker admits and defends "allowable" rhymes. "It may be objected," he says, "that a work of this kind contributes to extend poetical blemishes, by furnishing imperfect materials and apologies for using them. But it may be answered that, if these imperfect rhymes were allowed to be blemishes, it would still be better to tolerate them than cramp the imagination by the too narrow boundaries of exactly similar sounds." Now, it is perfectly true, of course, that a *poet* may well be allowed to effect the compromise of sacrificing a rhyme for a thought; but the versifier (for whom Walker's book is meant) must have no such license. He must learn to walk before he runs. Yet apart from this, Walker's argument is singularly illogical; there can be no need to catalogue the blemishes, even on the ground he urges, since the imagination would suggest the license, not the license stimulate the imagination. Walker's book, being simply mechanical, should have been confined to the correct machinery of verse, and imagination should have been allowed to frame for itself the licenses, which it would not dream of seeking in a hand-book.

[And here occasion serves to declare with emphasis that any theory of "allowable" rhymes is a rank heresy to which no one should give in now that the art of rhyming has been carried to its most varied perfection at the hands of yet living poets. Either two words rhyme together or they do not. The linking together in a couplet of "ever" and "river," of "shadow" and "meadow," of "heaven" and "driven," seen only

GUIDES AND HAND-BOOKS. 39

too often, is without excuse. Identity of sound is the only test of rhyme, and the "e" in "ever" is not pronounced like the "i" in "river," any more than the "a" in "shadow" sounds like the "ea" in "meadow."] The absurdity of talking of perfect and imperfect rhymes is only equaled by that of speaking of good grammar and bad grammar. A shilling is a shilling— what the vulgar call "a bad shilling" is no shilling at all.

But for this defect, Walker's Dictionary would be the best book of the sort possible. It contains, besides an index in which rhymes are arranged under various terminations, as in Bysshe's work, a terminational dictionary of three hundred pages; a dictionary, that is, in which the words are arranged as in ordinary dictionaries, save that the last and not the first letter of the word is that under which it is ranged.

Of the recent books published, there are but two of any note or importance in England. One claims to be a "complete practical guide to the whole subject of English versification"—"an exhaustive treatise," in which the writer, by way of simplifying matters, proposes to supersede the old titles of spondee, dactyl, etc., by the titles of "march," "trip," "quick," and "revert," and makes accents intelligible by calling them "backward" and "forward," with such further lucidities as "hover," "main," "midabout," and other technicalities afford. Its chief characteristic, however, is a decided condemnation of rhyme altogether, and a suggestion of the substitution of "assonance," under which "path" and "ways," and "pride" and "wife," would do duty for rhyme! The treatise, though spoiled by pedantic aiming after novelties of nomenclature, and too assertive language, is worth perusal. But as "a practical guide" it is at present useless, and will remain so until English rhyme is disestablished and disendowed by act of Parliament. Although its author modestly describes it as "the first treatise of the kind ever completed," and considers it "will in no mean degree serve to advance" the study of English verse, it is to be feared that there is little danger of its setting the Pierian spring on fire.

A more practical "Handbook of Poetry" is the best work of the kind I have met with, but it is full of grave errors. It begins with a definition of "Poetry," which makes it identical with "Verse," and it tends too much to the side of license in consequence, from the fact of permitting to the versifier freedoms which poets only can claim. On rhyme it is singularly inconsistent. It pronounces as no rhyme "heart" and "art," which to any but a cockney ear are perfect rhymes. Yet, a few paragraphs farther on, its only objection to the coupling of "childhood" and "wildwood" as a double rhyme, is that it is hackneyed; whereas it is not a double rhyme at all! In a chapter on "Imagery," though "metaphor" is catalogued, "simile" is omitted, and both together reappear under the needless subdivision "tropes." An anthology is added, and a dictionary of double and treble rhymes—as if it were possible to give anything like an exhaustive list of them in twenty pages!

Such being the imperfections, whether of short-

GUIDES AND HAND-BOOKS. 41

coming or excess, of the various existing hand-books, I venture to hope that this little treatise may plead some excuse for its appearance. It does not pretend to be an exhaustively complete practical guide or handbook to poetry. It is simply an attempt to set forth simply but strictly the Rules of Rhyme.

[Two American books, published since the English author wrote, demand notice here. The first is "A Vocabulary of English Rhymes," by the Rev. Samuel W. Barnum (D. Appleton & Co., 1876). This is by far the most elaborate, logical, and exact of rhyming dictionaries. Its only defect is that it is perhaps a little severe in the arrangement by vowel-sounds, and that it gives in to the heresy of allowable rhymes. But it is a useful book for the student. The second is the late Sidney Lanier's "Science of English Verse" (Charles Scribner's Sons, 1880), in which he lays the foundations of verse on the physical laws of sound. The "Science of Verse" is not easy reading, but it will well repay careful study; in it, for the time, verse is examined from the proper and scientific point of view. It is emphatically a book for the student to ponder after he has read Poe's essay.]

CHAPTER IV.

OF FEET AND CÆSURA.

THE feet most often met with in English verse are those corresponding with the trochee and iambus,* that is approximately. The iambic is most common, perhaps, represented by two syllables with the accent on the last syllable. The trochee has two syllables, with the accent on the first. An example of a line in each meter will show the difference :

Four Foot Iambic.
" To fair' Fide'le's gras'sy tomb'."

Four Foot Trochaic.
" Not' a sin'gle man' depart'ed."

Dactyls (an accented followed by two unaccented syllables) and anapæsts (two unaccented syllables followed by an accented one) are most frequently used in combination with the other feet :

Anapæstic.
" O'er the world' | from the hour' | of her birth'."

---

* The spondee (two long syllables) can have no equivalent in accent, as it would need two accented syllables next to each other, which can only be used very exceptionally.—(T. H.)

Dactylic.

"Make' no deep | scru'tiny
In'to her | mu'tiny."

It appears to me preferable to retain the classic names for these feet, rather than to try and invent new titles for them. One writer on versification has attempted to do this, and calls the iambic "march" measure, and the trochaic "trip." This seems to me to render the nature of the measure liable to misconstruction, as if the former only suited elevated themes, and the latter light ones; whereas the meter of Hudibras is iambic, and Aytoun's ballad of the "Battle of Flodden" is trochaic. The truth is, that the form of the foot has little to do with the "march" or "trip" of the verse, for "The Bridge of Sighs" is written in a dactylic form; and, according to the authority just alluded to, if the trochee be a "trip," the dactyl must be a "jig"!

By the combinations of these feet in certain numbers a line is constituted. Those in which two, three, and four feet occur—dimeters, trimeters, and tetrameters—are not so general as lines of more feet, and in these latter a new feature has to be recognized and provided for—the cæsura or pause. Strictly, the cæsura causes poetry to be written in lines, the end of each being a cæsura; but there are other cæsuras in the line, one or more according to its length. In the best verse they correspond with a natural pause in the sense of the words. When they do not, the artificial punctuation injures the harmony with which the sound and the sense should flow together. It is by varying the fall of the cæsura that the best writers of blank decasyllabic verse contrive to divest it of monotony. In some of the more irregular forms of verse, especially when it is unrhymed, the cæsura is all-important, giving to the lines their rise and fall—a structure not altogether unlike what has been termed the parallelism of Hebrew versification.

It is scarcely possible to lay down rules for the use of the cæsura, or pause, in English verse. It differs from the classic cæsura in falling at the end of both foot and word. Of its possible varieties we may gain some idea when we note that, in the decasyllabic line, for instance, it may fall after each foot, and it is by the shifting of its place that in this, as in blank verse, monotony is avoided. In shorter measures, especially of a lyric nature, it generally falls midway in the line.

The plan of giving to our accentual feet the titles given to the classical quantitative feet has been strongly condemned by some writers. I venture to think they have hardly considered the matter sufficiently. It must be better to use these meaningless terms (as we use the gibberish of Baroko and Bramantip in logic) than to apply new names which, by aiming at being expressive, may be misleading. But there is something more than this to be considered. There is in accent this, in common with quantity, that just as two shorts make a long, and can be substituted for it, so two unaccented syllables may take the place of one rather more accented; or perhaps it will be found that the substitution is due less to the correspondence in accent alone than

OF FEET AND CÆSURA.

to correspondence of quantity as well as accent. To put it briefly, these resolutions of the foot into more syllables are—like similar resolutions in music—a question of time, and time means quantity rather than accent. As an instance of this, I may give the much-quoted, often-discussed line :

"Than tired eyelids upon tired eyes."

The ordinary method of scanning this is to make a dissyllable of "tired," as if it were "ti-erd," a vulgarism of which its author would never have been guilty. The truth is, that the long "i" and the roll of the "r" correspond in time to a dissyllable, and, by changing the run of the line, carry out perfectly Pope's notion of the sound echoing the sense.

These resolutions, therefore, need a most accurate ear, and no slight experience. The versifier will do well, as a beginner, to refrain from attempting them. When he has gone on writing verse by rule of thumb until he begins to discover a formality in them that would be the better for variation, he may fairly try his hand at it—but not until then. Before that, his redundancy of syllables would be the result of faulty or unfinished expression, not the studied cause of a change in run.

CHAPTER V.

METER AND RHYTHM.

IT was scarcely possible to explain what the feet in verse are without assuming the existence of lines, in order to give intelligible examples of the various feet. But the consideration of the construction of lines really belongs to this chapter.

A line is composed of a certain number of feet, from two to almost any number short of ten or so—if indeed we may limit the number exactly, for there is nothing to prevent a man from writing a line of twenty feet if he have ingenuity enough to maintain the harmony and beat necessary to constitute verse. As a rule, we seldom meet with more than eight feet in a line.

A line may consist of feet of the same description, or of a combination of various feet. And this combination may be exactly repeated in the corresponding line or lines, or one or more of the feet may be replaced by another corresponding in time or quantity. Here is an instance:

"I knew | by the smoke that so gracefully curled . . .
And I said | 'if there's peace to be found in the world.'"

METER AND RHYTHM.

Here the iambic "I knew'" is resolved into the anapæst, "and I said'," *—or rather (as the measure is anapæstic) the iambic takes the place of the anapæst.

When only two feet go to a line, it is a dimeter. Three form a trimeter, four a tetrameter, five a pentameter, six a hexameter, seven a heptameter, eight an octameter, which, however, is usually resolved into two tetrameters. If the feet be iambics or trochees, of course the number of syllables will be double that of the feet—thus a pentameter will be decasyllabic. When dactyls or anapæsts are used, of course the number of syllables exceeds the double of the feet. But there is no necessity for enlarging on this point: I have given enough to explain terms, with which the student may perhaps meet while reading up the subject of versification. As he may also meet with the terms "catalectic" and "acatalectic," it may be as well to give a brief explanation of them also. A catalectic line is one in which the last foot is not completed. An acatalectic is one in which the line and the foot terminate together. An extract from the "Bridge of Sighs," a dactylic poem, will illustrate this:

"Make no deep | scrutiny
Into her | mutiny;

---

* In the classic measures a long (-) is equivalent to two short (⌣) quantities, in the English feet it is the unaccented syllables (which we may rudely consider the shorts) which are capable of resolution. In spite of this difference, however, it seems most simple to keep the old terms, and use the old formulæ.—(T. H.)

Rash and un | dutiful,
Past all dis | honor;
Death has left | on her
· Only the | beautiful.

. . . .

Take her up | tenderly,
Lift her with | care;
Fashion'd so | slenderly,
Young and so | fair."

Here the fourth and fifth, the eighth and tenth lines are catalectic. In the first two the last foot needs one syllable, in the others it requires two. It is scarcely necessary to point out how such variations improve and invigorate the measure, by checking the gallop of the verse.

We have now seen that the line may be composed of various numbers of the different feet. The next step to consider is the combination of lines into stanzas.

Stanzas are formed of two or more lines. Two lines are styled a couplet, three a triplet, and four a quatrain, while other combinations owe their titles to those who have used them first or most, as in the case of the Spenserian stanza.

The reader will see at once that, each of these kinds of stanzas being constructible of any of the styles of line before enumerated, each style of line being in its turn constructible of any of the sorts of feet described in a previous chapter, to make any attempt to give an exhaustive list of stanzas would be to enter upon an arithmetical progression alarming to think of.* I shall therefore only enumerate a few, giving, as seems most useful for my purpose, examples of the most common form of a peculiar stanza, as in the case of the decasyllabic couplet of Pope, and the nine-line stanza of Spenser, or the least common, as when, in the quatrain, it appears preferable to give, instead of the alternate-rhymed octosyllabic tetrameters which have been repeated *ad nauseam,* such fresh forms as will be found in the extracts from "The Haunted House," or Browning's "Pretty Woman."

EXAMPLES.

THE COUPLET OR DISTICH.†

Dimeter (four-syllabled).

"Here, here I live
And somewhat give."
—*Herrick, Hesperides.*

Tetrameter (eight-syllabled).

"His tawny beard was th' equal grace
Both of his wisdom and his face."
—*Butler, Hudibras.*

---

* Various forms of stanza may be combined in one poem (though most usually in the ode only), provided regard be had to harmony and unity, so that the meters be not varied unsuitably or violently.—(T. H.)

† In couplets, the two lines, in triplets (with two exceptional forms) the three, rhyme together. In quatrains usually the alternate lines rhyme. As the lines of the stanza increase in number, the methods of rhyming of course vary.—(T. H.)

Tetrameter (seven-syllabled).
"As it fell upon a day
In the merry month of May."
—*Shakespeare.*

Pentameter (ten-syllabled, "Pope's decasyllable").
"Truth from his lips prevail'd with double sway,
And fools who came to scoff remained to pray."
—*Goldsmith, Deserted Village.*

Hexameter (twelve-syllabled).
"Doth beat the brooks and ponds for sweet refreshing soil:
That serving not—then proves if he his scent may foil."
—*Drayton, Polyolbion.*

Heptameter (fourteen-syllabled).
"Now glory to the Lord of Hosts, from whom all glories are;
And glory to our sovereign liege, King Henry of Navarre."
—*Macaulay, Battle of Ivry.*

The couplet may also be formed of two lines of irregular length:

"Belovëd, O men's mother, O men's queen!
Arise, appear, be seen."
—*Swinburne, Ode to Italy.*

"Where the quiet-colored end of evening smiles
Miles on miles."
—*Browning, Love among the Ruins.*

"Morning, evening, noon, and night,
'Praise God,' sang Theocrite."
—*Browning, The Boy and the Angel.*

"Take the cloak from his face and at first
Let the corpse do its worst."
—*Browning, After.*

"Or for a time we'll lie
As robes laid by."
—*Herrick, Hesperides.*

"Give me a cell
To dwell."
—*Herrick, Hesperides.*

Two couplets are at times linked together into a quatrain. More often they are formed into six-line stanzas—that is, a couplet followed by a line which has its rhyme in another line following the second couplet. But, indeed, the combination of stanzas is almost inexhaustible.

TRIPLETS.

Trimeter (six-syllabled).

"And teach me how to sing
Unto the lyric string
My measures ravishing."
—*Herrick, Hesperides.*

Tetrameter (seven-syllabled).

"O, thou child of many prayers,
Life hath quicksands, life hath snares,
Care and age come unawares."
—*Longfellow, Maidenhood.*

Octameter (fifteen-syllabled).

"Was a lady such a lady, cheeks so round and lips so red—
On her neck the small face buoyant, like a bell-flower o'er its bed,

O'er the breast's superb abundance where a man might
　　base his head."
　　　　　　　　—*Browning, A Toccata.*

The triplet pure and simple is not a very common form; it is most frequently combined with other forms to make longer stanzas. At times the second line, instead of rhyming with the first or third, finds an echo in the next triplet—sometimes in the second, but more often in the first and third lines:

　　" Make me a face on the window there,
　　　Waiting, as ever mute the while,
　　　My love to pass below in the square.

　　" And let me think that it may beguile
　　　Dreary days, which the dead must spend
　　　Down in their darkness under the aisle."
　　　　　　　—*Browning, The Statue and the Bust.*

Another species of triplet occurs in the Pope measure (pentameter-decasyllabic). It is formed by the introduction, after an ordinary couplet, of a third line, repeating the rhyme, and consisting of eleven syllables and six feet. Dryden, however, and some other writers, gave an occasional triplet without the extra foot. The Alexandrine—i. e., the six-foot line—ought to close the sense, and conclude with a full stop.

THE QUATRAIN.

Of this form of stanza the name is legion. Of the most common styles, the reader's memory will supply numerous examples. I shall merely give a few of the rarer kinds. The quatrain may consist practically of two couplets, or of a couplet divided by a couplet, as in Tennyson's "In Memoriam." But the usual rule is to rhyme the first and third, and second and fourth. The laxity which leaves the two former unrhymed is a practice which can not be too strongly condemned. Quatrains so formed should in honesty be written as couplets; but such a condensation would possibly not suit the views of the mob of magazine versifiers, who have inflicted this injury, with many others, upon English versification.

It may be well to note here that the rhyme of the first and third lines should be as dissimilar as possible in sound to that of the second and fourth. This is, in fact, a part of the rule which forbids repetitions of the same vowel-sounds in a line—chief of all, a repetition of the particular vowel-sound of the rhyme. The rhymes recurring give a beat which is something like a cæsura, and when, therefore, the rhyme sound occurs elsewhere than at its correct post, it mars the flow. Here follow a few examples of the quatrain. I have not specified the syllables or feet, as the reader by this time will have learned to scan for himself; and, owing to the varieties of measure, such a specification would be cumbrous:

"The woodlouse dropp'd and roll'd into a ball,
    Touch'd by some impulse, occult or mechanic,
And nameless beetles ran along the wall
    In universal panic."
                    —*Hood, Haunted House.*

> "That fawn-skin-dappled hair of hers,
>   And the blue eye,
>   Dear and dewy,
> And that infantine fresh air of hers."
> —*Browning, A Fair Woman.*

> "All thoughts, all passions, all delights,
>   Whatever stirs this mortal frame;
> All are but ministers of love,
>   And feed his sacred flame."
> —*Coleridge, Love.*

> "What constitutes a state?
> Not high-raised battlement or labor'd mound,
>   Thick wall, or moated gate,
> Nor cities proud with spires and turrets crown'd."
> —*Jones, Ode.*

> "Whither, midst falling dew,
> While glow the heavens with the last steps of day,
> Far through their rosy depths, dost thou pursue
>   Thy solitary way."
> —*Bryant, To a Waterfowl.*

> "Sweet day, so calm, so cool, so bright,
>   The bridal of the earth and sky,
>   The dews shall weep thy fall to-night,
>   For thou must die."
> —*Herbert, Virtue.*

THE FIVE-LINE STANZA.

I am inclined to think this one of the most musical forms of the stanza we possess. It is capable of almost endless variety, and the proportions of rhymes, three

METER AND RHYTHM.

and two, seem to be especially conducive to harmony. It would be curious to go into the question how many popular poems are in this form. Here are two examples—both of them from favorite pieces:

> "Go, lovely rose,
> Tell her that wastes her time and me,
> That now she knows
> When I resemble her to thee,
> How sweet and fair she seems to be."
> —*Waller, To a Rose.*

> "Higher still and higher
> From the earth thou springest;
> Like a cloud of fire,
> The blue deep thou wingest,
> And singing still dost soar, and soaring ever singest."
> —*Shelley, The Skylark.*

[A third may be added, from a dashing American poem:

> "Hark! the jingle
> Of the sleigh-bells' song!
> Earth and air in snowy sheen commingle;
> Swiftly throng
> Norseland fancies, as we sail along."
> —*Stedman, The Sleigh-Ride.*]

Mr. Browning frequently uses this stanza, and with admirable effect. Although he has been accused of ruggedness by some critics, there is no modern poet who has a greater acquaintance with the various forms of verse, or can handle them more ably. The following are examples of his treatment:

"Is it your moral of life?
　Such a web, simple and subtle,
Weave we on earth here, in impotent strife
　Backward and forward each throwing his shuttle—
Death ending all with a knife?"
　　　　　　　　　　—*Master Hugues.*

"And yonder at foot of the fronting ridge,
　That takes the turn to a range beyond,
Is the chapel, reach'd by the one-arch'd bridge,
　Where the water is stopp'd in a stagnant pond,
Danced over by the midge."
　　　　　　　　　　—*By the Fireside.*

"Stand still, true poet that you are!
　I know you; let me try and draw you.
Some night you'll fail us; when afar
　You rise, remember one man saw you—
Knew you—and named a star."
　　　　　　　　　　—*Popularity.*

"Not a twinkle from the fly,
　Not a glimmer from the worm.
When the crickets stopp'd their cry,
　When the owls forbore a term,
You heard music—that was I!"
　　　　　　　　　　—*A Serenade.*

"When the spider to serve his ends,
　　By a sudden thread,
　　Arms and legs outspread,
On the table's midst descends—
Comes to find God knows what friends!"
　　　　　　　　　　—*Mesmerism.*

THE SIX-LINE STANZA.

With the increasing number of lines comes an increasing number of combinations of rhymes. There is the combination of three couplets, and there is that of two couplets, with another pair of rhymes, one line after the first, the other after the second couplet. Then there is a quatrain of alternate rhymes, and a final couplet—to mention no others :

> " Fear no more the heat o' the sun,
>   Nor the furious winter's rages ;
> Thou thy worldly task hast done,
>   Home art gone, and ta'en thy wages—
> Golden lads and girls all must
> Like chimney-sweepers come to dust."
> —*Shakespeare.*

> " One day, it matters not to know
> How many hundred years ago,
> A Spaniard stopt at a posada door ;
>   The landlord came to welcome him and chat
>   Of this and that,
> For he had seen the traveller here before."
> —*Southey, St. Romuald.*

> " And wash'd by my cosmetic brush,
> How Beauty's cheeks began to blush
>   With locks of auburn stain—
> Not Goldsmith's Auburn, nut-brown hair
> That made her loveliest of the fair,
>   Not loveliest of the plain."
> —*Hood, Progress of Art.*

"Some watch, some call, some see her head emerge
Wherever a brown weed falls through the foam;
Some point to white eruptions of the surge—
But she is vanish'd to her shady home,
Under the deep inscrutable, and there
Weeps in a midnight made of her own hair."
—*Hood, Hero and Leander.*

"Ever drifting, drifting, drifting,
  On the shifting
Currents of the restless heart—
Till at length in books recorded,
  They like hoarded
Household words no more depart."
—*Longfellow, Seaweed.*

"Before me rose an avenue
  Of tall and sombrous pines;
Abroad their fanlike branches grew,
And where the sunshine darted through,
  Spread a vapor, soft and blue,
  In long and sloping lines."
—*Longfellow, Prelude.*

["Might we but hear
The hovering angels' high imagined chorus,
 Or catch betimes, with wakeful eyes and clear,
One radiant vista of the realm before us—
 With one rapt moment given to see and hear,
      Ah! who would fear?"
   —*Stedman, The Undiscovered Country.*]

The following form may be looked upon as Burns's exclusively:

> "Wee, modest, crimson-tipped flower—
> Thou'st met me in an evil hour,
> For I maun crush among the stour
>   Thy slender stem ;
> To spare thee now is past my power,
>   Thou bonnie gem."
>   —*To a Mountain Daisy.*

THE SEVEN-LINE STANZA.

This form is not very common. It may be formed of a quatrain and triplet; of a quatrain, a line rhyming the last of the quatrain, and a couplet ; of a quatrain, a couplet, and a line rhyming the fourth line. Or these may be reversed.

THE EIGHT-LINE STANZA.

This is susceptible of endless variety, commencing with two quatrains, or a six-line stanza and a couplet, or two triplets with a brace of rhyming lines, one after each triplet.

> " Thus lived—thus died she ; nevermore on her
>   Shall sorrow light or shame. She was not made
> Through years or moons the inner weight to bear,
>   Which colder hearts endure till they are laid
> By age in earth ; her days and pleasures were
>   Brief but delightful ; such as had not staid
> Long with her destiny. But she sleeps well
> By the sea-shore whereon she loved to dwell."
>   —*Byron, Don Juan.*

THE NINE-LINE STANZA.

Of this form the most generally used is the Spenserian, or the following variation of it:

> " A little, sorrowful, deserted thing,
>   Begot of love and yet no love begetting ;
>   Guiltless of shame, and yet for shame to wring ;
>   And too soon banish'd from a mother's petting
>   To churlish nature and the wide world's fretting,
>   For alien pity and unnatural care ;
>   Alas ! to see how the cold dew kept wetting
>   His childish coats, and dabbled all his hair
>   Like gossamers across his forehead fair."
>   —*Hood, Midsummer Fairies.*

The Spenserian has the same arrangement of the rhymes, but has an extra foot in the last line. The two last lines of a stanza from "Childe Harold" will illustrate this :

> " To mingle with the universe and feel
>   What I can ne'er express, yet can not all conceal."
>   —*Byron.*

The formation of the ten, eleven, twelve, etc., line stanzas is but an adaptation of those already described. A single fourteen-line stanza of a certain arrangement of rhyme is a sonnet [which is considered in a special chapter]. I am almost inclined to omit discussion of blank verse, but will give a brief summary of its varieties. The ordinary form of blank verse is the decasyllabic in which Milton's " Paradise Lost " is written:

> "Of man's first disobedience and the fruit
> Of that forbidden tree whose mortal taste
> Brought death into the world and all our woe."

This consists of ten syllables with an accented following an unaccented syllable. It is preserved from monotony by the varying fall of the cæsura or pause. It occurs but rarely after the first foot or the eighth foot, and not often after the third and seventh. Elisions and the substitution of a trisyllable, equivalent in time for a dissyllable, are met with, and at times the accent is shifted, when by the change the sense of the line gains in vigor of expression, as in

> "Once found, which yet unfound, most would have thought Impossible."

According to scansion "most would'," but by the throwing back of the accent strengthened and distinguished into "*most* would have thought." In addition to this, in the blank verse of the stage, we find occasionally additional syllables, as

> "Or to take arms against a sea of troub(les)."

Other forms of blank verse follow :

1. "If aught of oaten stop or pastoral song
    May hope, chaste Eve, to soothe thy modest ear,
    Like thy own solemn springs,
    Thy springs and dying gales."
    —*Collins, Ode to Evening.*

2. "But never could I tune my reed
    At morn, or noon, or eve, so sweet,

As when upon the ocean shore
    I hail'd thy star-beam mild."
—*Kirke White, Shipwrecked Solitary's Song.*

3.   "Who at this untimely hour
Wanders o'er the desert sands?
No station is in view,
No palm-grove islanded amidst the waste—
The mother and her child,
The widow'd mother and the fatherless boy,
They at this untimely hour
Wander o'er the desert sands."*
—*Southey, Thalaba.*

4.   "Friend of my bosom, thou more than a brother,
Why wast not thou born in my father's dwelling?
So might we talk of the old familiar faces."
—*Lamb.*

5.   "See how he scorns all human arguments
So that no oar he wants, nor other sail
Than his own wings between so distant shores." †
—*Longfellow, Translation of Dante.*

6.   "Yet dost thou recall
Days departed, half-forgotten,
When in dreamy youth I wander'd
By the Baltic."
—*Longfellow, To a Danish Song-Book.*

7.   "All things in earth and air
Bound were by magic spell

---

* See also Shelley's "Queen Mab."—(T. H.)
† This is the simple decasyllable, the peculiarity being a division into stanzas of three lines.—(T. H.)

Never to do him harm;
Even the plants and stones,
All save the mistletoe,
The sacred mistletoe."
—*Longfellow, Tegner's Drapa.*

8. "Give me of your bark, O birch-tree!
Of your yellow bark, O birch-tree!
Growing by the rushing river,
Tall and stately in the valley."
—*Longfellow, Hiawatha.*

9. "Heard he that cry of pain; and through the hush that succeeded
Whisper'd a gentle voice, in accents tender and saintlike,
'Gabriel, oh, my beloved!' and died away into silence."
—*Longfellow, Evangeline.*

An extremely musical form of blank verse, the trochaic, will be found in Browning's "One Word More":

"I shall never in the years remaining,
Paint you pictures, no, nor carve you statues,
Make you music that should all-express me;
So it seems; I stand on my attainment:
This of verse alone one life allows me;
Verse and nothing else have I to give you.
Other heights in other loves, God willing—
All the gifts from all the heights, your own, love!"

This by no means exhausts the varieties of blank verse; but, as I have already said, blank verse is, on the whole, scarcely to be commended to the student for practice, because it is, while apparently the easiest, in reality the most difficult form he could attempt. It is in fact particularly easy to attain the blankness—but the verse is another matter. The absence of rhymes necessitates the most perfect melody and harmony, if the lines are to be anything beyond prose chopped up into lengths.

There are, I should mention before closing this chapter, many more styles of stanza than I have named, and many varieties of them. The ode is of somewhat irregular construction, but it is, I consider, beyond the scope of those for whom this book is intended, and it needs not to be considered on that account.

[Those who seek a discussion of its origin and form may be referred to the excellent volume of "English Odes," selected and edited by Mr. Edmund W. Gosse. This volume is included in the series of "English Classics," now appearing at irregular intervals. It contains a preface, all too brief, wherein the ode is described and criticised with the erudition of a scholar and the sympathy of a poet.]

CHAPTER VI.

OF RHYME.

A RHYME must commence on an accented syllable. From the accented vowel of that syllable to the end, the two or more words intended to rhyme must be identical in sound; but the letters preceding the accented vowel must in each case be dissimilar in sound. Thus "learn," "fern," "discern," are rhymes, with the common sound of "ern" preceded by the dissimilar sounds of "l," "f," "sc." "Possess" and "recess" do not rhyme, having besides the common "ess" the similar pronunciation of the "c" and the double "s" preceding it. The letters "r" and "l," when preceded by other consonants, so as practically to form new letters, can be rhymed to the simple "r" and "l" respectively, thus "track" and "rack," "blame" and "lame," are rhymes. The same rule applies to letters preceded by "s," "smile" being a rhyme to "mile." Similarly "h" and its compound rhyme, e. g., "shows," "those," "chose," and any word ending in "phose" with "hose."

The aspirate to any but a Cockney would, of course, pass as constituting the needful difference at the beginning of a rhyme, as in "heart" and "art," "hair" and "air."*

Rhymes are single, double, or treble — or more properly one-syllabled, two-syllabled, and three-syllabled. Rhymes of four or more syllables are peculiar to burlesque or comic verse. Indeed, Dryden declared that only one-syllabled rhymes were suitable for grave subjects: but every one must have at his fingers' ends scores of proofs to the contrary, of which I will instance but one—"The Bridge of Sighs." [Perhaps an even better example is the magnificent mediæval hymn, the "Dies Iræ," which owes much of its might to the skillful employment of double rhymes.]

Monosyllables or polysyllables accented on the last syllable are "single" rhymes. Words accented on the penultimate or last syllable but one supply "double" rhymes; e. g., agitat'ed, elat'ed. When the accent is thrown another syllable back, and falls on the antepenultimate as in "ar'rogate," it is in the first place a "triple" rhyme. But, as in English there is a tendency to alternate the acute and grave accent, the trisyllable

---

* It is a curious confirmation of my theory about the Cockney grounds for objection to this rhyme, that the author of a hand-book, who condemns "heart" and "art" as a rhyme, fails to see any fault in "dawn" and "morn," or in "applaud" and "aboard" as rhymes. Of course, where the "h" is mute, as in "hour," it can not rhyme with the simple vowel as in "our," sound being the test of rhyme, and the ear the only judge. A "rhyme to the eye" is an impossibility. [And elsewhere the author aptly remarked that "the union of *sound* alone constitutes rhyme. You do not match colors by the nose, or sounds by the eye."]

has practically two rhymes, a three-syllabled and a one-syllabled — thus "arrogate" and "Harrogate" rhyme, but "arrogate" may also pair off with "mate." Nevertheless, it is necessary to be cautious in the use of words with this spurious accent — it is perhaps better still to avoid them. Such words as "merrily," "beautiful,"."purity," ought never to be used as single-syllabled rhymes; even such words as "merited" and "happiness" have a forced sound when so used.

Elisions should be avoided, though "bow'r" and "flow'r" may pass muster, with some others. "Ta'en," "e'er," "e'en," and such contractions may, of course, be used. The articles, prepositions, and such, can not in serious verse stand as rhymes, under the same rule which condemns the separation of the adjective from its substantive in the next line.

It is scarcely necessary to premise that to write verse decently the student must have a thorough knowledge of grammar. From ignorance on that score arise naturally blemishes enough to destroy verse, as they would poetry, almost. I have seen verses which, beginning by apostrophizing some one as "thou," slipped in a few lines into "yours" and "you"—or, worse still, have said "thou doeth," or "thou, who is."

Expletives and mean expressions also must be excluded. The verse should never soar to "highfalutin," or sink to commonplace language. Simplicity is not commonplace, and nobility is not "highfalutin," and they should be aimed at accordingly; when you have acquired the one, you will as a rule find the other in its company.

When three or more lines are intended to rhyme together, the common base or accented vowel in each instance must be preceded by a different sound. For example, "born," "corn," and "borne," will not serve for a triplet, because, though the first and third are both rhymes to the second, they are not rhymes to each other.

It is as well, unless you are thoroughly acquainted with the pronunciation of foreign languages, to abstain from using them in verse, especially in rhymes. I met with the following instance of the folly of such rhyming in a magazine, not long ago:

"Prim Monsieurs fresh from Boulogne's *Bois* . . .
For these the Row's a certain *draw*."

This is about as elegant as rhyming "Boulogne" and "Song."

It is wise—on the principle of rhyme, the difference of sounds preceding the common base—to avoid any similarity by combination. For example, "is" is a good rhyme for "'tis," but you should be careful not to let "it" immediately precede the "is," as it mars the necessary dissimilarity of the opening sound of the two rhymes.

Let the beginner remember one thing: rhyme is a fetter, undoubtedly. Let him therefore refrain from attempting measures with frequent rhymes, for experience alone can give ease in such essays. Only the skilled can dance gracefully in fetters. Moreover, a

OF RHYME.

too frequent repetition of rhyme at short intervals gives a jigginess to the verse. It is on this account that the use in a line of a sound similar to the rhyme should be avoided. This does not apply to the generous use of a rhyme at the half-line to mark the cæsural pause, as in this line:

" 'Twas in the prime of summer time."

Nor is there any objection—but rather the contrary—to the use of two rhyming words in a line, provided they are not identical with the final rhymes, as for example:

" That thrice the human span
Through *gale* and *hail* and fiery bolt
Had stood erect as man."

[There is a more unexpected and delightful use of this internal rhyme in one of Mr. Frederick Locker's charming " London Lyrics ":

" Arise then, and lazy
Regrets from thee fling,
For *sorrows* that hazy
To-*morrows* may bring!"]

As a final warning, let me entreat the writer of verses to examine his rhymes carefully, and see that they chime to an educated ear. Such atrocities as "morn" and "dawn," "more" and "sure," "light in" and "writing," "fought" and "sort," are fatal to the success of verse. They stamp it with vulgarity, as surely as the dropping of the "h" stamps a speaker. Furthermore, do not make a trisyllable of a dissyllable — as, for instance, by pronouncing "ticklish" "tick-el-ish," and if you have cause to rhyme "iron," try "environ" or "Byron," not "my urn," because only the vulgar pronounce it "iern," or "apron" "apern," etc.

[And as a final note it may be well to give a list of a few of the English words that have no rhyme :

Bilge,	Gulf,	Rhomb,
Chimney,	Have,	Scarce,
Coif,	Kiln,	Scarf,
Crimson,	Microcosm,	Silver,
Culm,	Month,	Widow,
Cusp,	Mouth (verb),	Window.]
Fugue,	Oblige,	

CHAPTER VII.

OF FIGURES.

THE figures most commonly used in verse are similes and metaphors. A simile is a figure whereby one thing is likened to another. It is ushered in by a "like" or an "as."

"Like sportive deer they coursed about."
—*Hood, Eugene Aram.*

"Such a brow
His eyes had to live under, clear as flint."
—*Browning, A Contemporary.*

"Resembles sorrow only
As the mist resembles rain."
—*Longfellow, The Day is Done.*

"Look how a man is lower'd to his grave . . .
So is he sunk into the yawning wave."
—*Hood, Hero and Leander.*

A metaphor is a figure whereby the one thing, instead of being likened to the other, is, as it were, transformed into it, and is described as doing what it (the other) does.

"Poetry is
The grandest chariot wherein king-thoughts ride."
—*Smith, Life Drama.*

"The anchor, whose giant hand
Would reach down and grapple with the land."
—*Longfellow, Building of the Ship.*

Sometimes the two are united in one passage, as in—

"The darkness
Falls from the wings of night,
As a feather is wafted downward."
—*Longfellow, The Day is Done.*

The last line is a simile, but "the wings of night" is metaphorical. "A simile," says Johnson, "to be perfect, must both illustrate and ennoble the subject; but either of these qualities may be sufficient to recommend it."

Alliteration, when not overdone, is an exquisite addition to the charm of verse. The Poet Laureate thoroughly understands its value. Mr. Swinburne allows it too frequently to run riot. Edgar Allan Poe carried it to extravagance. I select an example from each:

"The moan of doves in immemorial elms,
And murmur of innumerable bees."
—*Tennyson.*

"The lilies and languors of virtue,
For the raptures and roses of vice."
—*Swinburne, Dolores.*

> "Come up through the lair of the lion
> With love in her luminous eyes."
>
> —*Poe, Ulalume.*

The instance from the Poet Laureate is a strong one—the repetition of the "m" is to express the sound of the bees and the elms. The alternation in the others is only pleasing to the ear, and the artifice in the last instance certainly is too obvious. In the Poet Laureate's lines the alliteration is so ingeniously contrived that one scarcely would suppose there are as many as seven repetitions of the "m." In Poe's, one is surprised to find the apparent excess of alliteration is due to but four repetitions. But the "l's" are identical with the strongest beats in the line, whereas the "m's" in Tennyson's line are interspersed with other letters at the beats. He uses this artifice more frequently than those would suspect who have not closely examined his poems, for he thoroughly appreciates the truth of the maxim, *ars est celare artem*.* A few lines from "The Princess" will illustrate this:

> "The baby that by us,
> Half-lapt in glowing gauze and golden brede,
> Lay like a new-fall'n meteor on the grass,
> Uncared-for, spied its mother and began
> A blind and babbling laughter, and to dance
> Its body, and reach its fatling innocent arms
> And lazy ling'ring fingers."

---

* " 'Tis the highest art to hide all art."

Here a careful study will reveal alliteration within alliteration, and yet the effect is perfect, for there is no sign of labor.

Elision must be used with a sparing hand. Generally speaking, a vowel that is so slightly pronounced that it can be elided, as in "temperance"—"temp'rance," may just as well be left in, and accounted for by managing to get the "quantity" to cover it. Where it is too strongly pronounced, to cut it out is to disfigure and injure the line, as in the substitution of "wall'wing" for "wallowing." That elision is often used unnecessarily may be seen in the frequency with which, in reading verse, we—according to most authorities—elide the "y" of "many":

"Full many a flower is doom'd to blush unseen."—*Gray.*

Here we are told we elide the "y" of "many," and some would replace "flower" by "flow'r." Yet to the most sensitive ear these may receive, in reading, their share of pronunciation, without damage to the flow of the line, if the reader understands quantity. "To" is often similarly "elided," as in—

"Can he to a friend—to a son so bloody grow?"—*Cowley.*

On the other hand, it is as well not to make too frequent use of the accented "ed," as in "amazéd." In "belovéd" and a few more words it is commonly used, and does not, therefore, sound strange. In others it gives a forced and botched air to the verse.

In verse some latitude is allowed in arranging the order of words in a sentence, but it must not be indulged in too freely. A study of the style of our best poets is the only means of learning what is allowable and what is not; it is impossible to explain it within the limits of this treatise. It may, however, be laid down, as a first principle, that no change in the order of words is admissible, if it gives rise to any doubt as to their real meaning—for example, if you wish to say, "the dog bit the cat," although such an inversion of construction as putting the objective before and the nominative after the verb is allowed in verse, it is scarcely advisable to adopt it, and say, "the cat bit the dog." [In *vers de société* inversion is forbidden, as that kind of verse is supposed to be a rhyming of the clever talk of clever people—in which, of course, the cart would never be put before the horse. An inversion always gives a sense of constraint and conscious effort. Note how few inversions there are in Mr. Austin Dobson's "Vignettes in Rhyme."]

CHAPTER VIII.

OF BURLESQUE AND COMIC VERSE, AND
VERS DE SOCIETE.

IT will be as well for the reader to divest himself at once of the notion that verse of this class is the lowest and easiest form he can essay, or that the rules which govern it are more lax than those which sway serious composition. The exact contrary is the case. Comic or burlesque verse is ordinary verse *plus* something. Ordinary verse may pass muster if its manner be finished, but comic verse must have some matter as well. Yet it does not on that account claim any license in rhyme, for it lacks the gravity and importance of theme which may at times, in serious poetry, be pleaded as outweighing a faulty rhyme.

This style of writing needs skill in devising novel and startling turns of rhyme, rhythm, or construction, and can hardly be employed by those who do not possess some articulate wit or humor—that is to say, the power of expressing, not merely of appreciating those qualities.

A defective rhyme is a fault in serious verse—it is a crime in comic. It is no sin to be ignorant of Greek or Latin, but it is worse than a blunder, under such

OF BURLESQUE AND COMIC VERSE. 77

circumstances, to quote them, and quote them incorrectly. In the same way, one is not compelled to write comic verse; but if he does write it, and can not do so correctly, he deserves severe handling.

One of the leading characteristics of this style is dexterous rhyming—and the legerdemain must be effected with genuine coin, not dumps. In the very degree that clever composite rhyming assists in making the verse sparkling and effective, it must bear the closest scrutiny and analyzation—must be real Moët, not gooseberry.

All, then, that has been said with regard to serious verse applies with double force to the lighter form of *vers de société*. According to the definition of Mr. Frederick Locker, no mean authority, *vers de société* should be "short, elegant, refined, and fanciful, not seldom distinguished by chastened sentiment, and often playful. The tone should not be pitched high; it should be idiomatic, and rather in the conversational key; the rhythm should be crisp and sparkling, and the rhyme frequent, and never forced, while the entire poem should be marked by tasteful moderation, high finish, and completeness: *for, however trivial the subject-matter may be—indeed, rather in proportion to its triviality—subordination to the rules of composition, and perfection of execution, should be strictly enforced.*"

Let me entreat the reader to bear that italicized sentence in memory when writing any style of verse, but most especially when he essays the comic or burlesque.

No precedent for laxity can be pleaded because the poets who have at times indulged in such trifling have therein availed themselves of the licenses which they originally took out for loftier writing. *Non semper arcum tendit Apollo,* * and the poet may be excused for striking his lyre with careless fingers. But we, who do not pretend to possess lyres, must be careful about the fingering of our kits. Apollo's slackened bow offers no precedent for the popgun of the poetaster.

As I have already said, much of the merit of this style depends on the scintillations, so to speak, of its rhymes. They must therefore be perfect. When Butler wrote the much-quoted couplet :

"When pulpit, drum ecclesiastick,
Was beat with fist instead of a stick,"

he was guilty of coupling "astick" and "a stick" together as a rhyme, which they do not constitute. But he who on that account claims privilege to commit a similar offense, not only is guilty of the vanity of demanding to be judged on the same level as Butler, but is illogical. Two wrongs can not constitute a right, and all the bad rhyming in the world can be no extenuation of a repetition of the offense.

The results of carelessness in such matters are but too apparent! The slipshod that has been for so long suffered to pass for comic verse, has brought the art into disrepute. In the case of burlesque, this is even more plainly discernible. It is held in so small esteem that people have come to forget that it boasts Aristophanes as its founder! Halting measures, cockney rhymes, and mere play on sound, instead of sense, in

---

* " Apollo does not always bend the bow."

OF BURLESQUE AND COMIC VERSE. 79

punning, have gone near to being the death of what at its worst was an amusing pastime, at its best was healthy satire.

The purchase of half a dozen modern burlesques will account for the declining popularity of burlesque. *All* of them will be found defaced by defective rhymes, and cockneyisms too common to provoke a smile. In the majority of them the decasyllabic meter will be found to range from six or eight syllables to twelve or fourteen! Most bear the same relation to real burlesque-writing that the school-boy's picture of his master—a circle for head and four scratches for arms and legs—bears to genuine caricature. [Much of the success of Mr. W. S. Gilbert's comic operas is due to the variety of his verse, to the unexpectedness of his rhymes, and to the apt choice of musical rhythms.]

The most telling form of rhyme in comic versification is the polysyllabic, and the greater the number of assonant syllables in such rhymes the more effective they prove. The excellence is co-extensive, however, with the unexpectedness and novelty, and there is therefore but small merit in such a polysyllabic rhyme as—

"From Scotland's mountains down he came,
And straightway up to town he came."

This merely consists of the single rhymes "down" and "town," with "he came" as a common affix. Such polysyllabics may be admitted here and there in a long piece, but, when they constitute the whole or even a majority of the rhymes, the writer is imposing on his readers. He is swelling his balance at his banker's by adding noughts on the right hand of the pounds' figure without paying in the cash.

Another feature of this style of verse is the repetition of rhymes. Open the "Ingoldsby Legends," * which may be taken as the foundation of one school of comic verse, and you will scarcely fail to light upon a succession of rhymes, coming one after the other, like a string of boys at leap-frog, as if the well-spring of rhyme were inexhaustible.

Although punning scarcely comes within the scope of this treatise, it may not be amiss to remind those who may desire to essay comic verse, that a pun is a double-*meaning*. It is not sufficient to get two words that clink alike, or to torture by mispronunciation a resemblance in sound between words or combinations of words. There must be an echo in the sense—"a likeness in unlikeness" in the idea.

Proper names should not be used as rhymes. The only exception is in the case of any real individual of note—a statesman, author, or actor, when to find a telling rhyme to the name, a rhyme suggestive of the habits or pursuits of the owner of that name, has some merit, especially if the name be long and peculiar. But to introduce an imaginary name for the sake of a rhyme, is work that is too cheap to be good. A child can write such rhyme as—

"A man of strict veracity
  Was Peter James M'Assity."

---

* I would, however, warn the beginner not to adopt the license of loose rhyming, which in Barham is lost sight of amid the brightness of the wit.—(T. H.)

OF BURLESQUE AND COMIC VERSE.

In composite rhyming the greatest care should be taken to see that each syllable after the first is identical in sound in each line. In "use he was" and "juicy was," the "h" destroys the rhyme, and the difference in sound in the last syllable (however carelessly pronounced) between such words as "oakum" and "smoke 'em" has a similar disqualifying power. It is scarcely necessary to refer to such inadmissible couples as "protector" and "neglect her," "birching" and "urchin," "oracle" and "historical."

One trick in rhyming is often very effective, but it must not be put into force too often. In some instances, however, it tells with great comical effect, by affording a rhyme to a word which at first glance the reader thinks it is impossible to rhyme. Canning, in the "Anti-Jacobin," used it with ludicrous effect in Rogero's song, and a few lines from that will illustrate and explain the trick I allude to:

"Here doom'd to starve on water gru-
-el, never shall I see the U-
-niversity of Gottingen!"

Here the division of the words "gruel" and "University" has an extremely absurd effect. But the artifice must be used sparingly, and those who employ it must beware of one pitfall. The moiety of the word which is carried over to begin the next line must be considered as a fresh word occupying the first foot. There is a tendency to overlook it, and count it as part of the previous line, and that of course is a fatal error.

Parody may be considered as a form of comic versification. It is not enough that a parody should be in the same meter as the original poem it imitates. Nor is it sufficient that the first line or so has such a similarity as to suggest the original. In the best parodies each line of the original has an echo in the parody, and the words of the former are retained as far as possible in the latter, or replaced by others very similar.

Another form of parody is the parody of style, when, instead of selecting a particular poem to paraphrase, we imitate, in verse modeled on the form he usually adopts, the mannerisms of thought or expression for which any particular writer is distinguished.

Examples of both kinds of parody will be found in the "Rejected Addresses" of James and Horace Smith, which should be studied together with Hood, Barham, Wolcot, and Thackeray, by those who would read the best models of humorous, comic, or burlesque writing. I may add here that *vers de société* will be best studied in the writings of Praed, Prior, and Moore. From living writers it would be invidious to single out any, either as models or warnings. [Thus far had the author written eight years ago: to-day the editor feels he would be derelict to his duty did he not advise the student of *vers de société*—which are something more than mere "society verse"—of Dr. Holmes, Mr. E. C. Stedman, and Mr. Austin Dobson. More broadly comic verse is to be found in Mr. W. S. Gilbert's "Bab Ballads" and Mr. C. S. Calverley's "Fly Leaves." Nor should the poetry of Mr. Bret Harte be neglected.]

CHAPTER IX.

OF SONG-WRITING.

ALTHOUGH song-writing is one of the most difficult styles of versification, it is now held in but little repute, owing to the unfortunate condition of the musical world in England. "Any rubbish will do for music" is the maxim of the music shop-keeper, who is practically the arbiter of the art nowadays, and who has the interests he is supposed to represent so little at heart that he would not scruple to publish songs, consisting of "nonsense verses"—as school-boys call them—set to music, if he thought that the usual artifice of paying singers a royalty on the sale for singing a song would prevail on the public to buy them.

Another reason why "any rubbish will do for music" has passed into a proverb is, that few amateur singers—and not too many professionals—understand "phrasing." How rarely can one hear what the words of a song are! Go to a "musical evening" and take note, and you will see that, in nine cases out of ten, when a new song has been sung, people take the piece of music and look over the words. A song is like a cherry, and ought not to require us to make two bites at it.

Nor is the injury inflicted on music due only to the amount of rubbish which is made to do duty for songs. The writings of our poets are ransacked for "words," and accompaniments are manufactured to poems which were never intended, and are absolutely unfitted, for musical treatment. Then, because it is found that poems are not to be converted into songs so easily as people think, the cry is not merely that "any rubbish will do for songs," but that "*only* rubbish will do "—a cry that is vigorously taken up by interested persons.

The truth lies between the two extremes. A peculiar style of verse is required, marked by such characteristics and so difficult of attainment that some of our greatest poets—Byron for one—have failed as song-writers. English literature reckons but few really good song-writers. When you have named Moore, Lover, Burns, and Barry Cornwall, you have almost exhausted the list.

There is in the last edition of the works of the lamented writer I have just named—Samuel Lover—a preface in which he enters very minutely into the subject of song-writing. The sum of what he says is, that "the song being necessarily of brief compass, the writer must have powers of condensation. He must possess ingenuity in the management of meter. He must frame it of open vowels, with as few guttural or hissing sounds as possible, and he must be content sometimes to sacrifice grandeur or vigor to the necessity of selecting *singing* words and not *reading* ones." He adds that "the simplest words best suit song, but simplicity must not descend to baldness. There must be a thought in the song, gracefully expressed, and it must appeal either to the fancy or feelings, or both, but rather by suggestion than direct appeal; and philosophy and didactics must be eschewed."

He adduces Shelley, with his intense poetry and exquisite sensitiveness to sweet sounds, as an instance of a poet who failed to see the exact necessities of song-writing, and gives a quotation from one of Shelley's "songs" to prove this. The line is:

"The fresh earth in new leaves drest,"

and he says very pertinently, "It is a sweet line, and a pleasant image—but I defy any one to sing it: *nearly every word shuts up the mouth instead of opening it.*" That last sentence is the key to song-writing. I use the word song-writing in preference to "lyrical writing," because "lyrical" has been warped from its strict meaning, and applied to verse which was not intended for music. It is not absolutely necessary that a song-writer should have a practical knowledge of music, but it is all the better if he have: beyond doubt, Moore owed much of his success to his possession of musical knowledge.

CHAPTER X.

OF THE SONNET.

ANY discussion of the sonnet is handling a burning question. We are not at the threshold of the discussion by the query, What is a sonnet? And on the answer to this the whole discussion turns. A sonnet is a poem containing one, and only one, idea, thought, or sentiment, and consisting of fourteen lines of equal length—so much is admitted by all. There are those who consider any poem of fourteen lines a sonnet. There are others who declare that to be a true sonnet the poem must not only have fourteen lines of equal length, but its construction and the arrangement of its rhymes must conform to a prescribed pattern, called after Petrarch. Sonnets written in the Petrarchan or Guittonian form are "regular" or "correct"; all others are "irregular" and "incorrect." A regular sonnet consists of two quatrains (in which the 1st, 4th, 5th, and 8th lines rhyme together, and likewise the 2d, 3d, 6th, and 7th), followed by two tercets (in which the 9th, 11th, and 13th lines rhyme together, and likewise the 10th, 12th, and 14th), thus:

"FREDERICKSBURG.

"The increasing moonlight drifts across my bed,
  And on the churchyard by the road, I know,
  It falls as white and noiselessly as snow.
'Twas such a night two weary summers fled ;
The stars as now were waning overhead.
  Listen ! Again the shrill-lipped bugles blow
  Where the swift currents of the river flow
Past Fredericksburg ; far off the heavens are red
With sudden conflagration : on yon height,
  Linstock in hand, the gunners hold their breath ;
A signal-rocket pierces the dense night,
  Flings its spent stars upon the town beneath ;
Hark !—the artillery massing on the right,
  Hark !—the black squadrons wheeling down to death."
                        —T. B. Aldrich, Fredericksburg.

Mr. Waddington, in a "Note on the Sonnet," at the end of his collection of "English Sonnets by Living Writers" (London, 1881), tells us that about one third of Petrarch's sonnets are written in this form, and most of Ariosto's. But the arrangement most often adopted by the Italian poets has been to employ a fifth rhyme in the sestet, so that the 9th and 12th lines rhyme together, the 10th and 13th, and the 11th and 14th. Here is an admirable example :

"What is a sonnet ? 'Tis a pearly shell
    That murmurs of the far-off murmuring sea ;
    A precious jewel carved most curiously ;
  It is a little picture painted well.

What is a sonnet? 'Tis the tear that fell
    From a great poet's hidden ecstasy;
    A two-edged sword, a star, a song—ah me!
Sometimes a heavy-tolling funeral bell.
This was the flame that shook with Dante's breath,
    The solemn organ whereon Milton played,
    And the clear glass where Shakespeare's shadow
      falls:
A sea this is—beware who ventureth!
    For like a fiord the narrow floor is laid
      Deep as mid-ocean to sheer mountain walls."
                                —*R. W. Gilder.*

Strictly, these two forms only are entitled to be called "correct" and "regular." But even the purists are willing generally to allow variety in the sequence of rhymes in the sestet. It is the octave in which there must be no variation. So long as the sestet contains two or three rhymes, and does not end with a couplet, the sonnet is tolerated. In the following fine sonnet the divergence from the accepted form is so slight that it is forgiven:

"HOMER'S ODYSSEY.

" As one that for a weary space has lain
    Lulled by the song of Circe and her wine
    In gardens near the pale of Proserpine,
Where that Ægean isle forgets the main,
And only the low lutes of love complain,
    And only shadows of wan lovers pine.
    As such an one were glad to know the brine
Salt on his lips, and the large air again,

> So gladly from the songs of modern speech
> Men turn and see the stars, and feel the free
> Shrill wind beyond the close of heavy flowers,
> And through the music of the languid hours
> They hear, like ocean on a western beach,
> The surge and thunder of the Odyssey."
>
> —*A. Lang.*

As soon, however, as we abandon the arrangement of an octave turning on two rhymes and a sestet turning on two or three rhymes at will, we must give up all claim to regularity or correctness. To a purist Shakespeare's sonnets are not sonnets at all, however beautiful they may be as poems. They are "quatorzains," if you will—poems of fourteen lines, or, as Charles Lamb called them, "fourteeners"—but they are not "sonnets." However irregular the form, and however inferior to the true Guittonian arrangement, it has been sanctified by genius. What Shakespeare found fit for his use, no meaner man may deem inadequate. Yet we may agree with Mr. Waddington that the "Guittonian variation is the best, and few poets, after once having become accustomed to it, ever return to the looser construction and less frequent rhymes of the other forms." It is perhaps not hazardous to say that the strict sonnet is driving out the mere "fourteener." Most of the younger poets are purists, and it is well that this is so; but many of the elder American poets—notably Lowell and Mrs. Kemble—claim the utmost license; and even a poet as finished in form as Mr. Frederick Locker has written a lovely sonnet on the Shakespearean model:

"LOVE, TIME, AND DEATH.

" Ah me, dread friends of mine—Love, Time, and Death !
   Sweet Love, who came to me on sheeny wing,
And gave her to my arms—her lips, her breath,
   And all her golden ringlets clustering ;
And Time, who gathers in the flying years,
   He gave me all—but where is all he gave ?
He took my love and left me barren tears ;
   Weary and lone I follow to the grave.
There Death will end this vision half divine,
   Wan Death, who waits in shadow evermore,
And silent, ere he gave the sudden sign ;
   Oh, gently lead me through thy narrow door,
Thou gentle Death, thou trustiest friend of mine.
   Ah me, for Love will Death my love restore ?"
                                        —*Frederick Locker.*

For any further discussion of this pregnant subject, reference must be made to Leigh Hunt's volumes, to Mr. Tomlinson's book, to the two collections of Mr. Waddington, and to the full " Treasury of English Sonnets," by Mr. David M. Main.

CHAPTER XI.

OF THE RONDEAU AND THE *BALLADE*.

IT is curious to note that the only fixed and rigid form of verse which we English-speaking peoples have until lately been willing to adopt is the sonnet. It is almost equally curious to note that the first impetus toward the introduction of new forms came to us from France, a country where, until within the last half-century, verse has been as prim and precise, as empty and as soulless, as metrical prose by any possibility may be. But, under the inspiration of the romantic revival which marked the dying days and final downfall of the elder branch of the house of Bourbon, and especially under the influence of the extraordinary vigor and vitality of Victor Hugo's earlier verse and prose, the fresh young blood of France began to course through more poetic channels, inventing new forms to vent its new-found feeling, and filling old forms again with the current of new life. The young poets went back to the verses of the troubadours and *trouvères*, and to the metrical forms of the fourteenth century; they went, indeed, wherever they hoped to find a form or a suggestion of style suitable and worthy of modern reproduction and resuscitation; the stranger, the more exotic, the better. The *ballade* and the rondeau were brought again into favor. The English ballad, with its wealth of suggestiveness and lyric possibility, was fit, indeed, to the minds of young writers fresh from the first reading of "Notre-Dame de Paris." Hugo called one collection of his poems "Odes et Ballades"—though, as a critic objected, it contained neither odes nor *ballades*—for the French *ballade* is radically different from the English ballad; and it was the English lyric which Hugo had in mind, not the French form of verse. In spite of the tendency toward the Gothic, none of the involved meters of the German Minnesingers were, as far as we find on record, at any time imitated. But English legends and lyrics, and fashions of all kinds, found frequent copyists, even to the verge of affectation—M. Auguste Maquet, the collaborator of Dumas, called himself for a while Augustus MacKeat, and Théophile Dondée became for a season Philothée O'Neddy! These eccentricities slowly passed away, and the good they had clouded remained. French poetry to-day is more like poetry and less like Pope than it has been for several centuries. Hugo's example has been followed—nay, even improved, for "the master," as his followers affectionately call him, is, like other great geniuses, often careless, and the art of Théophile Gautier, and of Baudelaire, and of M. Théodore de Banville, is above all things finished and polished and perfect.

And to-day the inspiration which the French poets caught from their study of the early forms of French

OF THE RONDEAU AND BALLADE. 93

verse is beginning to be transmitted across the Channel to England, and we now and then see an English rondeau or *villanelle;* and the sight is ever welcome, for nothing makes surer the poet's hold on the mechanism of his art than the practice of new meters and the study of foreign forms. The impulse in favor of the rondeau and the *ballade*, and their less important relatives, the *rondel* and *villanelle*, given in France by M. Théodore de Banville, was in England due to Mr. Austin Dobson, who united to a precision and polish and point, as fine as M. de Banville's, a poetic faculty far superior. Although a scant attempt had been made now and again to write a *triolet* in English, it was not until Mr. Dobson took up these French forms seriously, and studied them and adapted them to the genius of our language and of our versification, that they made any impression on the public mind. Indeed, it was not until the publication, in the "Cornhill Magazine" of July, 1877, of Mr. E. W. Gosse's "Plea for Certain Exotic Forms of Verse," and until the appearance of Mr. Dobson's "Proverbs in Porcelain," a little later, that even professed students of poetry began to understand what a *ballade* was, and that it might be precisely the instrument for the expression of certain moods of a poet. After Mr. Dobson had written his first *ballade*, Mr. Swinburne wrote one, followed soon by Mr. Andrew Lang, Mr. E. W. Gosse, and Mr. W. E. Henley, in England, and by Mr. H. C. Bunner and others in America.

In the course of the past four years a many rondeaux and *ballades* have got themselves written, and the French forms are now fairly familiar to the public which cares for poetry. In fact, the stage of experiment has passed; it has been shown that these forms can be used in English; and the sole question now is whether they have shown themselves worth using. I think it can be asserted fairly that at least two of them have proved their case, and are entitled to a favorable verdict. These are the rondeau and the *ballade*, which bid fair to take their place in our poetic armory side by side with the sonnet.

Of course, it would be absurd to assert that there is yet a rondeau or a *ballade* equal to the best English sonnet—whatever that may be. It is, perhaps, even claiming too much to say that either form, as a form, is equal to the sonnet. But the sonnet has been acclimated in our language for three hundred years. As Mr. Austin Dobson has admirably put it, in the apt and alluring "Note on some Foreign Forms of Verse" which he contributed to Mr. W. Davenport Adams's "Latter-day Lyrics" (London, 1878), there were doubtless contemporary critics who, when the English sonnet was in leading-strings, "regarded it as a merely new-fangled Italian conceit, suitable enough for the fantastic gallantries of Provençal courts of love, but affording little or no room for earnest or serious effort. They could not see 'Avenge, O Lord, thy slaughter'd saints!' in the primitive essays of Surrey and Wyatt." Mr. Dobson went on to concede that "the majority of the forms now in question are not at present suited for, nor are they intended to rival the more approved national rhythms in, the treatment of grave and elevated themes. What is modestly advanced for some of them (by the present writer at least) is that they may add a new charm of buoyancy—a lyric freshness—to amatory and familiar verse, already too much condemned to faded measures and outworn cadences." A little further on, Mr. Dobson has a remark which more than justifies the space given to these forms in this new edition of a technical manual: " They have also a humbler and obscurer use. If, to quote the once-hackneyed but now too-much-forgotten maxim of Pope—

" 'Those move easiest that have learned to dance,'

what better discipline, among others, could possibly be devised for 'those about to versify' than a course of rondeaux, *triolets*, and *ballades*."

Oddly enough, the two forms which seem most useful, and most likely to remain in use in our language—the rondeau and the *ballade*—were both attempted in England as early as was the sonnet. At the coronation of King Henry IV, John Gower, the author of the "Confessio Amantis," presented his Majesty with a collection of fifty *ballades* in the Provençal manner "to entertain the court." Unfortunately, these were in French, else might we trace an older pedigree for the English *ballade* than for the English sonnet. Sir Thomas Wyatt introduced the true sonnet into England, and he also wrote rondeaux in English; whether he was the first to do so or not, we can not tell at this late day. In the next century, Charles Cotton, friend of that compleat angler Isaak Walton, wrote an ungallant rondeau, to be found in Dr. Guest's "History of English Rhythms." In the last century there are a few squibs in rondeau form in the "Rolliad." Then came Mr. Austin Dobson.

The word rondeau has been applied inaccurately in English to any poem in which the first words of the stanza were repeated at the end. The one specimen of this sort, which all may remember, is Leigh Hunt's brief and beautiful—

> " Jenny kissed me when we met,
>   Jumping from the chair she sat in ;
>   Time, you thief, who love to get
>   Sweets upon your list, put that in—
>   Say I'm weary, say I'm sad,
>   Say that health and wealth have missed me,
>   Say I'm growing old ; but add—
>   Jenny kissed me ! "

How far this is from the real form of the rondeau can readily be seen by comparing it with this transcription by Mr. Dobson of a French rondeau of Voiture's :

> "' YOU BID ME TRY.'
>
> " You bid me try, blue eyes, to write
>   A rondeau.   What !—forthwith ?—to-night ?
>   Reflect.   Some skill I have, 'tis true ;
>   But thirteen lines—and rhymed on two—
>   ' Refrain,' as well.   Ah, hapless plight !
>
> " Still, there are five lines—ranged aright.
>   These Gallic bonds, I feared, would fright
>   My easy Muse.   They did till you—
>   *You* bid me try !

"This makes them nine. The port's in sight;
'Tis all because your eyes are bright!
Now, just a pair to end with 'oo'—
When maids command, what can't we do?
Behold! the rondeau—tasteful, light—
You bid me try!"

Here the poet describes and exemplifies at once. From this it is seen that the rondeau has thirteen lines with but two rhymes, eight of one and five of the other, in a rigidly prescribed order, and that the first four syllables are repeated as an unrhymed refrain after the eighth line and again at the end. Here is another example:

"SLEEP.

"O happy Sleep! that bear'st upon thy breast
The blood-red poppy of enchanting rest,
Draw near me through the stillness of this place
And let thy low breath move across my face,
As faint winds move above a poplar's crest.

"The broad seas darken slowly in the west;
The wheeling sea-birds call from nest to nest;
Draw near and touch me, leaning out of space,
O happy Sleep!

"There is no sorrow hidden or confess'd,
There is no passion uttered or suppress'd,
Thou canst not for a little while efface;
Enfold me in thy mystical embrace,
Thou sovereign gift of God most sweet, most blest,
O happy Sleep!"
—*Ada Louise Martin.*

From these two examples the structure of the rondeau is made plain, and its difficulty also, which chiefly lies in the handling of the refrain. To learn the inner secret of the rondeau, said the writer of an anonymous article whose author we can not but suspect, "to give the refrain a new savor and fragrance at each repetition by some covert art of setting, and to make it seem the mere bubbling over, as it were, of the eighth and thirteenth lines—these are things which only the masters of the lyre can attain to." To give absolute variety to the refrain, a complete change of meaning at each recurrence is enjoined, and the liberty of something very like punning is allowed.

There is another and slightly different form of the rondeau, altogether less apt either for deep meaning or sportive jest; notwithstanding which it has been used by Villon and by Alfred de Musset. Here is an English example:

"VIOLET.

"Violet delicate, sweet,
  Down in the deep of the wood,
Hid in thy still retreat,
Far from the sound of the street,
  Man and his merciless mood :—

"Safe from the storm and the heat,
  Breathing of beauty and good
  Fragrantly, under thy hood,
      Violet.

"Beautiful maid discreet,
  Where is the mate that is meet,

> Meet for thee—strive as he could—
> Yet will I kneel at thy feet,
> Fearing another one should,
> Violet!"
> —*W. Cosmo Monkhouse.*

Plainly the rondeau lends itself readily to the exigencies of the English language, yet it yields in power and variety to the *ballade*, which is also based on the triple use of a refrain. Perhaps example should always precede exposition. Villon, that "voice out of the slums of Paris," wrote a rondeau now and then, but his great love was the *ballade;* and in his hands it is a wonderful instrument. No English version can do justice to his verse, but it is well to begin by quoting a *ballade* of his:

"BALLADE OF THINGS KNOWN AND UNKNOWN.

> "Flies in the milk I know full well:
> I know men by the clothes they wear:
> I know the walnut by the shell:
> I know the foul sky from the fair:
> I know the pear-tree by the pear:
> When things go well, to me is shown:
> I know who work and who forbear:
> I know all save myself alone.

> "I know the pourpoint by the fell:
> And by his gown I know the frère:
> Master from varlet can I tell:
> And nuns that cover up their hair:
> I know a swindler by his air,
> And fools that fat on cates have grown:
> Wines by the cask I can compare:
> I know all save myself alone.

> "I know how horse from mule to tell:
> I know the load each one can bear:
> I know both Beatrice and Bell:
> I know the hazards, odd and pair:
> I know of visions in the air:
> I know the power of Peter's throne
> And how misled Bohemians were:
> I know all save myself alone.
>
> "ENVOY.
>
> "Prince, I know all things: fat and spare,
> Ruddy and pale, to me are known;
> And Death that endeth all our care:
> I know all save myself alone.
> —*John Payne, from François Villon.*

From this we see that the *ballade* consists of three stanzas and a half-stanza, called an envoy, and generally addressed directly to some prince or power; that the rhymes and arrangement of the first stanza are repeated in the others; and that the refrain concludes all three stanzas and the envoy. Eight-line stanzas with only three rhymes, as above, are the most often seen; but ten-line stanzas using four rhymes are also permissible—as may be seen below:

> "BALLADE OF THE MIDNIGHT FOREST.
>
> "Still sing the mocking fairies as of old,
> Beneath the shade of thorn and holly-tree;
> The west wind breathes upon them, pure and cold,
> And wolves still dread Diana roaming free
> In secret woodland with her company.
> 'Tis thought the peasant's hovels know her rite

When now the wolds are bathed in silver light,
And first the moonrise breaks the dusky gray,
　Then down the dells with blown soft hair and bright,
And through the dim wood Dian threads her way.

" With water-weeds twined in their locks of gold
　　The strange cold forest-fairies dance in glee,
Sylphs over-timorous and over-bold
　　Haunt the dark hollows where the dwarf may be,
　　The wild red dwarf, the nixies' enemy ;
Then 'mid their mirth and laughter, and affright,
The sudden Goddess enters, tall and white,
With one long sigh for summers passed away ;
　The swift feet tear the ivy nets outright
And through the dim wood Dian threads her way.

" She gleans her silvan trophies ; down the wold
　　She hears the sobbing of the stags that flee
Mixed with the music of the hunting roll'd,
　　But her delight is all in archery,
　　And naught of ruth and pity wotteth she.
More than her hounds that follow on the flight :
The goddess draws a golden bow of night
And thick she rains the gentle shafts that slay,
　She tosses loose her locks upon the night,
And through the dim wood Dian threads her way.

" ENVOY.

" Prince, let us leave the din, the dust, the spite,
　The gloom and glare of towns, the plague, the blight ;
　　Amid the forest leaves and fountain spray
There is the mystic house of our delight,
　And through the dim wood Dian threads her way."
　　　—*Andrew Lang, after Théodore de Banville.*

Two other varieties are known. One is the double *ballade*, which is simply a *ballade* with six stanzas (all repeating the rhymes and arrangement of the first of either eight lines or ten), and with or without an envoy, as the poet pleases. And the other is the *ballade* with a double refrain, in which the fourth line of the first stanza (always of eight lines) is repeated in the other stanzas, while the envoy consists of two couplets in which both refrains occur in order. The typical French example of the *ballade* with two refrains is the "Frère Lubin" of Clément Marot, which has been translated by both Longfellow and Bryant, neither of whom has preserved the *ballade* form. Here is the best attempt at the *ballade* with two refrains, and one of the most blithesome and debonair poems of its author:

"THE BALLADE OF PROSE AND RHYME.

"When the ways are heavy with mire and rut,
  In November fogs, in December snows,
    When the north wind howls, and the doors are shut—
  There is place and enough for the pains of prose;
  But whenever a scent from the whitethorn blows,
    And the jasmine-stars to the lattice climb,
  And a Rosalind-face to the casement shows—
Then hey!—for the ripple of laughing rhyme!

" When the brain gets as dry as an empty nut,
  When the reason stands on its squarest toes,
    When the mind (like a beard) has a 'formal cut'—
  There is place and enough for the pains of prose;
  But whenever the May-blood stirs and glows,
    And the young year draws to the 'golden prime,'

And Sir Romeo sticks in his ear a rose—
Then hey!—for the ripple of laughing rhyme!

" In a theme where the thoughts have a pendant strut,
In a changing quarrel of 'Ayes' and 'Noes,'
In a starched procession of 'If' and 'But'—
There is place and enough for the pains of prose;
But whenever a soft glance softer grows,
And the light hours dance to the trysting-time,
And the secret is told 'that no one knows'—
Then hey!—for the ripple of laughing rhyme!

"ENVOY.

" In the work-a-day world—for its needs and woes,
There is place and enough for the pains of prose;
But whenever the May bells clash and chime,
Then hey!—for the ripple of laughing rhyme!"
—*Austin Dobson.*

The great secret of the *ballade* is the apt choice and adroit use of the refrain. First catch your refrain. Then tame it to do your bidding, until (as the anonymous writer already quoted says neatly) "it recur without the tedium of importunity and return with the certainty of welcome." The *ballade* with a double refrain is doubly difficult, for it demands two good refrains contrasting sharply, and setting each other off to advantage. M. de Banville warns the *ballade*-maker against making his stanzas four lines at a time, for the two halves will never join imperceptibly; they will always be broken-backed. Each stanza should be homogeneous, cast in one jet, welded at a white heat. The thought of the *ballade*, the central and primary idea, should be brought out in each stanza and emphasized in the refrain; and then packed compactly into the final epigram of the envoy; finally, by the fourth repetition of the refrain, driven home to the head.

All of Mr. Dobson's *ballades* will repay study with delight; the most of them may be found in the American edition of his collected poems called "Vignettes in Rhyme" (New York: Henry Holt & Co., 1880). In Mr. Andrew Lang's dainty and delightful little volume of "XXXII Ballades in Blue China" (London: Kegan Paul, Trench & Co., 1881), are to be found *ballades* of great variety and dexterity.

CHAPTER XII.

OF OTHER FIXED FORMS OF VERSE.

BEFORE taking up the other fixed forms of verse, it may be well to digress for a moment to consider the use of the refrain, upon the regular recurrence of which the *ballade* and the rondeau and most of the other forms are based. No artistic effect of verse, as Poe says, has been so universally employed. It is to be seen in the meaningless choruses of college and convivial songs, in the recurrent catch-lines of the old English and Scotch ballads, and in the quaint repetitions of their modern imitations, like the "Sister Helen" of Mr. Rossetti, and the other mediævalisms which Mr. C. S. Calverley has comically parodied:

"The farmer's daughter hath soft brown hair
   (*Butter and eggs and a pound of cheese*);
And I met with a ballad I can't say where,
   Which wholly consisted of lines like these."

In these instances the refrain existed with but slight usefulness. As Poe says, it is in a primitive condition; "as commonly used, the refrain, or burden, . . . depends for its impression upon the force of monotone—both in sound and thought. The pleasure is deduced solely from the sense of identity—of repetition. I resolved to diversify, and so heighten, the effect, by adhering, in general, to the monotone of sound, while I continually varied that of thought; that is to say, I determined to produce continuously novel effects, by the variation of the application of the refrain—the refrain itself remaining, for the most part, unvaried." Poe's success in the execution of this device, which is not as novel as he declares, can be seen in "The Raven" and also in "The Bells." The same effect is produced in satiric verse in the "Biglow Papers," where

> " John P
>   Robinson, he
> Says he wont vote for Governor B,"

and in the virile and noble stanzas, in which Mr. Stedman tells us that

> " John Brown,
>   Ossawotomie Brown,
> Saw his sons fall dead beside him, and between them laid
>   him down."

In both of these, as in Poe's "Raven," the refrain recurs at regular intervals, and almost unvaried in form, but with great variety in the application. And this is the principle of the *ballade* and the rondeau and the *rondel* and their fellows. The words of the refrain are as the laws of the Medes and Persians, which alter not, but the meaning of these words admits of as much variety as the poet can impart.

Closely allied to the rondeau are the *triolet* and the *rondel*. Here is a *triolet:*

"A PITCHER OF MIGNONETTE.

"A pitcher of mignonette,
 In a tenement's highest casement:
Queer sort of a flower-pot—yet
That pitcher of mignonette
Is a garden in heaven set,
 To the little sick child in the basement—
The pitcher of mignonette,
 In the tenement's highest casement.
       —*H. C. Bunner.*

Thus we see that the *triolet* is a single stanza of two rhymes and eight lines, of which the first is repeated as the fourth, and the first and second as the seventh and eighth. "The *triolet* is, perhaps, best adapted for epigram," says a writer from whom I have already quoted; "the weight of its *raison d'être* rests on the fifth and sixth lines, while the perfection of its execution lies in the skill with which the third line is connected with the fourth, and the final couplet with the one preceding it."

The *rondel*, of which the earliest English examples were perhaps written by Charles of Orleans during his residence in England, is also closely akin to the rondeau. It is a poem of two rhymes and fourteen lines, with a repetition of the first and second lines as the seventh and eighth, and again as the thirteenth and fourteenth.

"READY FOR THE RIDE.

"Through the fresh fairness of the Spring to ride,
 As in the old days when he rode with her,
With joy of Love that had fond Hope to bride,
 One year ago had made her pulses stir.

"Now shall no wish with any day recur
   (For Love and Death part year and year full wide),
   Through the fresh fairness of the Spring to ride,
As in the old days when he rode with her.

"No ghost there lingers of the smile that died
   On the sweet pale lip where his kisses were—
. . . Yet still she turns her delicate head aside,
   If she may hear him come, with jingling spur—
Through the fresh fairness of the Spring to ride,
   As in the old days when he rode with her."
                    —*H. C. Bunner.*

It is, however, allowable at times to omit the fourteenth line and to end with the repetition of the first line as the thirteenth, thus:

"THE WANDERER.

"Love comes back to his vacant dwelling—
   The old, old Love that we knew of yore!
   We see him stand by the open door,
With his great eyes sad, and his bosom swelling.

"He makes as though in our arms repelling
   He fain would lie, as he lay before;
   Love comes back to his vacant dwelling—
The old, old Love which we knew of yore!

"Ah, who shall help us from over-spelling
   That sweet forgotten, forbidden Lore!
   E'en as we doubt, in our heart once more,
With a rush of tears to our eyelids welling,
Love comes back to his vacant dwelling!"
                    —*Austin Dobson.*

OF OTHER FIXED FORMS OF VERSE.

Just as the *rondel* and the *triolet* seem variations of the rondeau, so is the *chant-royal* a development of the *ballade*: it is to be defined roughly as a ballade of five stanzas of eleven lines, with an envoy of five lines. It is said that, according to the strict rule of the older French writers, the *chant-royal* should be an allegory, the solution of which is contained in the envoy. There are but few English *chants-royals*, for the making of them is a hard and thankless task. Mr. Gosse has written a splendidly sustained *chant-royal* to the "Praise of Dionysus," and Mr. Dobson another suggested by the "Death of Death." In America, so far as I know, but one has been written; and it is this one which I quote, for it shows how readily even the most difficult form lends itself to satire and humor:

"BEHOLD THE DEEDS!

[Being the Plaint of Adolphe Culpepper. Ferguson, Salesman of Fancy Notions, held in durance of his Landlady for a failure to connect on Saturday night.]

I.

"I would that all men my hard case might know;
  How grievously I suffer for no sin:
I, Adolphe Culpepper Ferguson, for lo!
  I of my landlady am lockéd in,
For being short on this sad Saturday,
Nor having shekels of silver wherewith to pay:
  She has turned and is departed with my key;
  Wherefore, not even as other boarders free,
    I sing (as prisoners to their dungeon-stones
  When for ten days they expiate a spree):
Behold the deeds that are done of Mrs. Jones!

II.

"One night and one day have I wept my woe ;
   Nor wot I, when the morrow doth begin,
If I shall have to write to Briggs & Co.,
   To pray them to advance the requisite tin
For ransom of their salesman, that he may
Go forth as other boarders go alway—
   As those I hear now flocking from their tea,
   Led by the daughter of my landlady
      Piano-ward. This day, for all my moans,
Dry bread and water have been servéd me.
   Behold the deeds that are done of Mrs. Jones!

III.

" Miss Amabel Jones is musical, and so
   The heart of the young he-boardér doth win,
Playing ' The Maiden's Prayer,' *adagio*—
   That fetcheth him, as fetcheth the banco skin
The innocent rustic. For my part, I pray:
That Badarjewska maid may wait for aye
   Ere sits she with a lover, as did we
   Once sit together, Amabel ! Can it be
      That all that arduous wooing not atones
For Saturday shortness of trade dollars three ?
   Behold the deeds that are done of Mrs. Jones!

IV.

" Yea ! she forgets the arm was wont to go
   Around her waist. She wears a buckle, whose pin
Galleth the crook of the young man's elbów.
   I forget not, for I that youth have been.
Smith was aforetime the Lothario gay.
Yet once, I mind me, Smith was forced to stay
   Close in his room. Not calm, as I, was he ;

But his noise brought no pleasaunce, verily.
Small ease he gat of playing on the bones
Or hammering on his stove-pipe, that I see.
Behold the deeds that are done of Mrs. Jones!

V.

" Thou, for whose fear the figurative crow
I eat, accursed be thou and all thy kin!
Thee will I show up—yea, up will I show
Thy too thick buckwheats, and thy tea too thin.
Ay! here I dare thee, ready for the fray:
Thou dost *not* 'keep a first-class house,' I say!
It does not with the advertisements agree.
Thou lodgest a Briton with a puggaree,
And thou hast harbored Jacobses and Cohns,
Also a Mulligan. Thus denounce I thee!
Behold the deeds that are done of Mrs. Jones!

" ENVOY.

" Boarders! the worst I have not told to ye:
She hath stolen my trowsers, that I may not flee
Privily by the window. Hence these groans.
There is no fleeing in a *robe de nuit*.
Behold the deeds that are done of Mrs. Jones!
—*H. C. Bunner.*

The *villanelle*, like the *rondel*, rondeau, and *triolet*, has but two rhymes; its peculiarity is the alternation of two refrains. It consists of five triplets, followed by a quatrain. The opening line is repeated as the third of the second and fourth triplets, and as the final line of the concluding quatrain. The third line reappears at the end of the third and fifth triplets, and as the next to last of the poem. The first and third lines of each triplet all rhyme together; and the second lines rhyme with one another. The following graceful example is not absolutely exact in form, as the poet has willfully, and without warrant, varied the last line, which ought to be absolutely identical with the third:

"There are roses white, there are roses red,
   Shyly rosy, tenderly white;
Which shall I choose to wreathe my head?

"Which shall I cull from the garden-bed
   To greet my love on this very night?
There are roses white, there are roses red.

"The red should say what I would have said;
   Ah! how they blush in the evening light!
Which shall I choose to wreathe my head?

"The white are pale as the snow new spread,
   Pure as young eyes and half as bright;
There are roses white, there are roses red.

"Roses white, from the heaven dew-fed,
   Roses red for a passion's plight,
Which shall I choose to wreathe my head?

"Summer twilight is almost fled,
   Say, dear love! have I chosen right?
There are roses white, there are roses red,
   All twined together to wreathe my head."
                  —*L. S. Bevington, Roses.*

It was supposed at one time that the *villanelle* might be of indefinite length, but the best authorities now agree with M. Boulmier that, as Passerat devised the form, it is fitting that his "J'ai perdu ma tourterelle" should be followed, and *that* consists of five triplets and a quatrain.

Something like the villanelle in its repetition of two lines, but without any limitation on the number of the stanzas, is the *pantoum*. Not content with merely French forms of verse, the French poets have even adopted one Malayan form, the *pantoum*, first brought to their attention in the notes to Hugo's "Orientales," and afterward employed to advantage by Théophile Gautier and M. Théodore de Banville. It is not at first sight encouraging; it consists of a series of four-line stanzas, the second and fourth lines of each stanza reappearing as the first and third of the next stanza, and so on *ad infinitum*, the first and third lines of the first stanza appearing again in the final one. Mr. Dobson's *pantoum* is a little long, so only beginning and end are here given:

"IN TOWN.
"'*The blue-fly sung in the pane.*'—TENNYSON.
" June in the zenith is torrid
 (There is that woman again !);
 Here, with the sun on one's forehead,
 Thought gets dry in the brain.

" There is that woman again ;
 'Strawberries! fourpence a pottle!'
 Thought gets dry in the brain ;
 Ink gets dry in the bottle.

" 'Strawberries! fourpence a pottle!'
 Oh, for the green of a lane!
 Ink gets dry in the bottle ;
 'Buzz' goes a fly in the pane!

"Some muslin-clad Mabel or May
    To dash one with eau de Cologne;
Bluebottle's off and away,
    And why should I stay here alone?

"To dash one with eau de Cologne
    All over one's talented forehead!
And why should I stay here alone?
    June in the zenith is torrid!"

There are very few *pantoums* in English, and not likely to be many more, for the writing of them is merely a freak of literary ingenuity, and not likely to have results of permanent value. There is an American *pantoum*, "En Route," in "Scribner's" for July, 1878, setting forth the misery of railroad travel in hot weather. In both "In Town" and "En Route" there is an attempt to make the constant repetitions not merely tolerable, but subservient to the general effect of monotonously recurrent sound—in the one case, the buzzing of the fly, and in the other, the rattle and strain of the cars.

The *sestina* is even more complicated and difficult than the *pantoum* or the *chant-royal*. It was invented by Arnauld Daniel, a Provençal troubadour of the end of the thirteenth century; and from him it was copied by various Italian, Spanish, and Portuguese poets. It consists of six six-lined stanzas, each of which ends with the same six words, not rhyming, but arranged in a prescribed order, and it concludes with an envoy of three lines, containing all six of the final words, three

OF OTHER FIXED FORMS OF VERSE. 115

at the end of the lines, and three in the body of the lines. I know only one English example of this form:

> "*Fra tutti il primo Arnaldo Daniello*
> *Gran maestro d'amor.*"—PETRARCH.

"In fair Provence, the land of lute and rose,
Arnaut, great master of the lore of love,
First wrought sestines to win his lady's heart,
For she was deaf when simpler staves he sang,
And for her sake he broke the bonds of rhyme,
And in this subtler measure hid his woe.

"'Harsh be my lines,' cried Arnaut, 'harsh the woe,
My lady, that enthorn'd and cruel rose,
Inflicts on him that made her live in rhyme!'
But through the meter spake the voice of Love,
And like a wild-wood nightingale he sang
Who thought in crabbed lays to ease his heart.

"It is not told if her untoward heart
Was melted by the poet's lyric woe,
Or if in vain so amorously he sang;
Perchance through cloud of dark conceits he rose
To nobler heights of philosophic love,
And crowned his later years with sterner rhyme.

"This thing alone we know : the triple rhyme
Of him who bared his vast and passionate heart
To all the crossing flames of hate and love,
Wears in the midst of all its storm of woe—
As some loud morn of March may bear a rose—
The impress of a song that Arnaut sang.

"'Smith of his mother-tongue,' the Frenchman sang
Of Launcelot and of Galahad, the rhyme

> That beat so blood-like at its core of rose,
> It stirred the sweet Francesca's gentle heart
> To take that kiss that brought her so much woe,
> And sealed in fire her martyrdom of love.
>
> " And Dante, full of her immortal love,
> Stayed his dear song, and softly, fondly sang
> As though his voice broke with that weight of woe;
> And to this day we think of Arnaut's rhyme
> Whenever pity at the laboring heart
> On fair Francesca's memory drops the rose.
>
> " Ah! sovereign Love, forgive this weaker rhyme!
> The men of old who sang were great at heart,
> Yet have we too known woe, and worn thy rose."
>
> —*E. W. Gosse, Sestina.*

A contemporary French poet, M. de Gramont, has adapted this Provençal form to more modern French versification. He began by making the six final words rhyme by threes, and he changed the rhythm from hendecasyllabics to Alexandrines. The form he thus modified he has used freely himself, and he has been followed by a few French poets and by the one English poet who has shown the greatest power of conquering rebel rhythms.

> " I saw my soul rest upon a day
>   As a bird sleeping in the nest of night,
> Among soft leaves that give the starlight way,
>   To touch its wings but not its eyes with light;
> So that it knew as one in visions may,
>   And knew not as men waking of delight.

" This was the measure of my soul's delight ;
   It has no power of joy to fly by day,
Nor part in the large lordship of the light,
   But in a secret, moon-beholden way
Had all its will of dreams and pleasant night,
   And all the love and life that sleepers may.

" But such life's triumph as men waking may
   It might not have to feed its faint delight
Between the stars by night and sun by day,
   Shut up with green leaves and a little light ;
Because its way was as a lost star's way,
   A world's not wholly known of day or night.

" All loves, and dreams, and sounds, and gleams, of night
   Made it all music that such minstrels may,
And all they had they gave it of delight ;
   But in the full face of the fire of day
What place shall be for any starry light,
   What part of heaven in all the wide sun's way ?

" Yet the soul woke not, sleeping by the way,
   Watched as a nursling of the large-eyed night,
And sought no strength nor knowledge of the day,
   Nor closer touch conclusive of delight,
Nor mightier joy, nor truer than dreamers may,
   Nor more of song than they nor more of light.

" For who sleeps once and sees the secret light
   Whereby sleep shows the soul a fair way
Between the rise and rest of day and night,
   Shall care no more to fare as all men may,
But be his place of pain or of delight,
   There shall he dwell, beholding night as day.

> "Song, have thy day and take thy fill of light
> Before the night be fallen across thy way;
> Sing while he may, man hath no long delight."
> —A. C. Swinburne, *Sestina.*

In French "light" and "delight" are admirable rhymes, but in English they are not rhymes at all. Perhaps Mr. Swinburne, having taken a French form, thought himself justified in following the French practice of rhyming. From Mr. Gosse's poem and from Mr. Swinburne's the secret of the construction of the sestina may be learned. The most obvious rule is that each stanza has at the end of its first line the final word of the preceding stanza. Then the second line terminates with the final word of the first line of the preceding stanza. And so the final words are chosen alternately from the last three lines and the first three lines of the stanza preceding. The whole subject, and indeed all the forms treated in this and the two chapters before, can best be studied in M. de Gramont's "Les Vers Français et leur Prosodie" (Paris: Hetzel), and in M. de Banville's "Petit Traité de Poésie Française" (Paris, Charpentier, 1881).

A FIT OF RHYME AGAINST RHYME.

Rhyme, the rack of finest wits,
That expresseth but by fits
      True conceit,
Spoiling senses of their treasure,
Cozening judgment with a measure,
      But false weight;
Wresting words from their true calling;
Propping verse for fear of falling
      To the ground;
Jointing syllables, drowning letters,
Fastening vowels, as with fetters
      They were bound!
Soon as lazy thou wert known,
All good poetry hence was flown,
      And art banished;
For a thousand years together,
All Parnassus green did wither,
      And wit vanished.

Pegasus did fly away;
At the wells no Muse did stay,
   But bewailed.
So I see the fountain dry,
And Apollo's music die,
   All light failed.
Starveling rhymes did fill the stage—
Not a poet in an age,
   Worthy crowning;
Not a work deserving bays,
Nor a line deserving praise,
   Pallas frowning.
Greek was free from rhyme's infection;
Happy Greek, by this protection,
   Was not spoiled;
Whilst the Latin, queen of tongues,
Is not yet free from rhyme's wrongs,
   But rests foiled.
Scarce the hill again does flourish,
Scarce the world a wit doth nourish,
   To restore
Phœbus to his crown again,
And the Muses to their brain,
   As before.
Vulgar languages that want
Words and sweetness and be scant
   Of true measure,

A FIT OF RHYME AGAINST RHYME.

Tyrant rhyme hath so abused
That they long since have refused
    Other censure.
He that first invented thee,
May his joints tormented be,
    Cramped for ever;
Still may syllables jar with time,
Still may reason war with rhyme,
    Resting never!
May his sense, when it would meet
The cold tumor in his feet,
    Grow unsounder;
And his title be long Fool,
That in rearing such a school
    Was the founder.
        —Ben Jonson.

DICTIONARY OF RHYMES.

A

AB, or ABB.

As in *cab*. Bab, cab, dab, Mab, gab, nab, blab, crab, drab, scab, stab, slab, St. Abb.

As in *squab*. See OB.

ABE.

Babe, astrolabe.

AC.

Zodiac, maniac, demoniac, ammoniac, almanac, symposiac, hypochondriac, aphrodisiac, crack, lac, brach, back, hack, bric-à-brac, jack, lack, pack, quack, tack, sack, rack, black, clack, crack, knack, slack, snack, stack, track, wrack, attack, smack, thwack, arrack.

ACE.

Ace, dace, pace, face, lace, mace, race, brace, chace, grace, place, Thrace, space, trace, apace, deface, efface, disgrace, displace, misplace, embrace, grimace, interlace, retrace, populace, carapace, base, case, abase, debase, vase.

ACH.
See ATCH.

ACHE.
See AKE.

ACS.
See AX.

ACT.
Act, fact, fract, pact, tract, attract, abstract, extract, tact, intact, contact, compact, contract, subact, co-act, detract, distract, exact, protract, enact, infract, subtract, transact, retract, re-act, cataract, counteract, the preterites and participles of verbs in ACK.

AD, or ADD.
As in *bad.* Add, bad, dad, gad, fad, had, lad, mad, pad, sad, brad, clad, glad, plaid (?), cad, chad, shad, etc.

As in *wad.* See OD.

ADE.
Cade, fade, made, jade, lade, wade, blade, bade, glade, shade, spade, trade, degrade, evade, dissuade, invade, persuade, blockade, brigade, estrade, arcade, esplanade, cavalcade, cascade, cockade, crusade, masquerade, renegade, retrograde, serenade, gambade, brocade, ambuscade, cannonade, palisade, rhodomontade, aid, maid, raid, braid, lemonade, staid, upbraid, afraid, and the preterites and participles of verbs in AY, EY, and EIGH. (The word *pomade* still retains the French *ade*, and rhymes with huzzaed, psha'd, baad.)

ADGE.

Badge, cadge.

ADZE.

Adze, rhymes plural of nouns, or third person singular present of verbs, in AD, ADD.

AEN.

Ta'en. See AIN.

AFE.

Safe, chafe, vouchsafe, waif, Ralph.

AFF.

Gaff, chaff, draff, graff, quaff, staff, distaff, engraff, epitaph, cenotaph, paragraph, photograph, telegraph, behalf, laugh, half, calf.

AFT.

Aft, haft, raft, daft, waft, craft, shaft, abaft, graft, draft, ingraft, handicraft, draught, and the preterites and participles of verbs in AFF and AUGH, etc.

AG.

Bag, cag, fag, gag, hag, jag, lag, nag, quag, rag, sag, tag, wag, brag, crag, drag, flag, knag, shag, snag, stag, swag, scrag, Brobdingnag.

AGD.

Smaragd, preterites and participles of verbs in AG.

AGE.

Age, cage, gage, mage, page, rage, sage, wage, stage, swage, assuage, engage, disengage, enrage, presage, appanage, concubinage, heritage, hermitage, parentage, personage, parsonage, pasturage, patronage, pilgrimage, villanage, equipage, and gauge.

AGM.

Diaphragm, rhymes AM.

AGNE.

Champagne. See AIN.

AGUE.

Plague, vague.

AH.

Ah, bah, shah, pah.

AI.

Serai, almai, ai, papai, ay.

AID.

See ADE.

AIGHT.

See ATE.

AIGN.

See ANE.

AIL.

Bail, brail, fail, grail, hail, jail, mail, nail, pail, quail, rail, sail, shail, tail, wail, flail, frail, snail, trail, assail, avail, detail, bewail, entail, prevail, aventail, wassail, retail, countervail, curtail, Abigail, ale, bale, dale, gale, hale, male, pale, sale, tale, vale, wale, scale, shale, stale, swale, whale, wale, impale, exhale, regale, veil, nightingale.

AIM.

See AME.

AIN.

Cain, blain, brain, chain, fain, gain, grain, lain, main, pain, rain, vain, wain, drain, plain, slain, Spain, stain, swain, train, twain, sprain, strain, abstain, amain, attain, complain, contain, constrain, detain, disdain, distrain, enchain, entertain, explain, maintain, ordain, pertain, obtain, refrain, regain, remain, restrain, retain, sustain, appertain, thane, Dane, bane, cane, crane, fane, Jane, lane, mane, plane, vane, wane, profane, hurricane, deign, arraign, campaign, feign, reign, vein, rein, skein, thegn, champagne.

AINST.

Against, rhymes abbreviated second person singular present of verbs in AIN, ANE, EIN, EIGN, AIGN.

AIQUE.

Caique. See AKE.

AINT.

Ain't, mayn't, faint, plaint, quaint, saint, taint, teint, acquaint, attaint, complaint, constraint, restraint, distraint, feint.

AIR and AIRE.

See ARE.

AIRD.
Laird rhymes preterites and participles of verbs in ARE.

AIRN.
Bairn, cairn.

AISE.
See AZE.

AISLE.
Aisle. See ILE.

AIT.
See ATE.

AITH.
Faith, wraith, rath, baith.

AIZE.
See AZE.

AK.
Dâk rhymes ALK.

AKE.
Ake, bake, cake, hake, lake, make, quake, rake, sake, take, wake, brake, drake, flake, shake, snake, stake, strake, spake, awake, betake, forsake, mistake, partake, overtake, undertake, bespake, mandrake, break, steak, ache, alcaic, caique, opaque.

AL.
Shall, pal, mall, sal, gal, fal-lal, cabal, canal, animal, admiral, cannibal, capital, cardinal, comical, conjugal,

corporal, criminal, critical, festival, fineal, funeral, general, hospital, interval, liberal, madrigal, literal, magical, mineral, mystical, musical, natural, original, pastoral, pedestal, personal, physical, poetical, political, principal, prodigal, prophetical, rational, satirical, reciprocal, rhetorical, several, temporal, tragical, tyrannical, carnival, schismatical, whimsical, arsenal, and many others.

ALD.

Bald, scald, rhymes the preterites and participles of verbs in ALL, AUL, and AWL.

ALE.

See AIL.

ALF.

See AFF.

ALK.

Balk, chalk, stalk, talk, walk, calk, dâk, squauk, baulk, caulk, catafalque, hawk, auk.

ALL.

All, ball, call, gall, caul, haul, Gaul, appal, enthral, awl, bawl, brawl, crawl, scrawl, sprawl, shawl, squall, hall, mawl, stall, fall, pall, tall, wall, install, forestall, thrall.

ALM, ALMS.

Calm, balm, becalm, psalm, palm, embalm; plurals and third persons singular rhyme with ALMS, as alms, calms, becalms, etc.

ALP.
Scalp, Alp.

ALQUE.
Catafalque. See ALK.

ALSE.
False, valse.

ALT.
As in *halt*. Halt, malt, exalt, salt, vault, assault, default, and fault.
As in *shalt*. Asphalt, alt, shalt.

ALVE.
As in *calve*. Calve, halve, salve.
As in *valve*. Valve, alve.

AM and AMB.
Am, dam, ham, pam, ram, Sam, cram, dram, flam, sham, swam, kam, clam, epigram, anagram, damn, lamb, jam, jamb, oriflamb, ma'am, telegram, lamm.

AME.
Blame, came, dame, same, flame, fame, frame, game, lame, name, prame, same, tame, shame, inflame, became, defame, misname, misbecame, overcame, aim, claim, maim, acclaim, declaim, disclaim, exclaim, proclaim, reclaim.

AMM.
Lamm. See AM.

AMME.

Oriflamme. See AM.

AMN.

Damn. See AM.

AMP.

As in *camp*. Camp, champ, cramp, damp, stamp, vamp, lamp, clamp, decamp, encamp.
As in *swamp*. Swamp, pomp, romp.

AN.

As in *ban*. Ban, can, Dan, fan, man, Nan, pan, ran, tan, van, bran, clan, plan, scan, span, than, unman, foreran, began, trepan, courtesan, partisan, artisan, pelican, caravan, shandydan, barracan.
As in *wan*. Wan, swan. See ON.

ANCE.

Chance, dance, glance, lance, trance, prance, intrance, romance, advance, mischance, complaisance, circumstance, countenance, deliverance, consonance, dissonance, extravagance, ignorance, inheritance, maintenance, temperance, intemperance, exorbitance, ordinance, concordance, sufferance, sustenance, utterance, arrogance, vigilance, expanse, enhance, France. [Here the *ance* is pronounced differently by different people, ănce and ānce.]

ANCH.

Branch, staunch, launch, blanch, haunch, paunch, ganch.

AND.

As in *band*. And, band, hand, land, rand, sand, brand, bland, grand, gland, stand, strand, command, demand, countermand, disband, expand, withstand, understand, reprimand, contraband, and preterites and participles of verbs in AN.

As in *wand*. Wand. See OND.

ANE.
See AIN.

ANG.

Bang, fang, gang, hang, pang, tang, twang, sang, slang, rang, harangue, swang, stang, lang, chang, clang.

ANGE.

Change, grange, range, strange, estrange, arrange, exchange, interchange.

ANGUE.

Harangue, rhymes ANG.

ANK.

Yank, bank, rank, blank, shank, clank, dank, drank, slank, frank, spank, stank, brank, hank, lank, plank, prank, rank, thank, disrank, mountebank.

ANSE.
See ANCE.

ANT.

As in *ant*. Ant, cant, chant, grant, pant, plant, rant, slant, aslant, complaisant, displant, enchant, gallant, implant, recant, supplant, transplant, absonant, adamant, arrogant, combatant, consonant, cormorant, protestant, significant, visitant, covenant, dissonant, disputant, elegant, elephant, exorbitant, conversant, extravagant, ignorant, insignificant, inhabitant, militant, predominant, sycophant, vigilant, petulant, can't, shan't, aunt, haunt.

As in *want*. Want, upon't, font.

AP.

As in *cap*. Cap, dap, gap, hap, lap, map, nap, pap, rap, sap, tap, chap, clap, trap, fap, flap, knap, slap, snap, wrap, scrap, strap, enwrap, entrap, mishap, affrap, mayhap.

As in *swap*. Swap. See OP.

APE.

Ape, cape, shape, grape, rape, scape, scrape, escape, nape, chape, trape, jape, crape, tape, etc.

APH.

See AFF.

APSE.

Apse, lapse, elapse, relapse, perhaps, and the plurals of nouns and third persons singular present tense of verbs in AP.

APT.

Apt, adapt. Rhymes the preterites and participles of verbs in AP.

AQUE.

Opaque. See AKE.

AR.

As in *bar*. Czar, bar, car, far, jar, mar, par, tar, spar, scar, star, char, afar, debar, petar, unbar, catarrh, particular, perpendicular, secular, angular, regular, popular, singular, titular, vinegar, scimetar, calendar, avatar, cinnabar, caviare, are.

As in *war*. See OR.

ARB.

Barb, garb, rhubarb.

ARCE.

Farce, parse, sarse, sparse. (*Scarce* has no rhyme.)

ARCH.

As in *march*. Arch, march, larch, parch, starch, countermarch.

As in *hierarch*. Hierarch, heresiarch. See ARK.

ARD.

As in *bard*. Bard, card, guard, hard, lard, nard, shard, yard, basilard, bombard, discard, regard, interlard, retard, disregard, and the preterites and participles of verbs in AR.

As in *ward*. Ward, sward, afford, restored, etc.

ARE.

As in *bare*. Care, dare, fare, gare, hare, mare, pare, tare, ware, flare, glare, scare, share, snare, spare, square, stare, sware, yare, prepare, aware, beware, compare, declare, ensnare, air, vair, fair, hair, lair, pair, chair, stair, affair, debonnair, despair, impair, glaire, repair, etc.; bear, pear, swear, tear, wear, forbear, forswear, etc.; there, were, where, ere, e'er, ne'er, elsewhere, whate'er, howe'er, howsoe'er, whene'er, where'er; heir, coheir, their.

As in *are*. Rhymes AR.

ARES.

Unawares. Rhymes theirs, and the plurals of nouns and third persons singular of verbs in are, air, eir, ear.

ARF.

Dwarf, wharf. (*Scarf* has no rhyme.)

ARGE.

Barge, charge, large, marge, targe, discharge, o'ercharge, surcharge, enlarge.

ARK.

Ark, bark, cark, clark, dark, lark, mark, park, chark, shark, spark, stark, embark, remark, hierarch, heresiarch.

ARL.

Carl, gnarl, snarl, marl, harl, parle.

ARM.

As in *arm*. Arm, barm, charm, farm, harm, alarm, disarm.

As in *warm*. Warm, swarm. See ORM.

ARN.

As in *barn*. Barn, yarn, tarn, darn.
As in *warn*. Warn, forewarn. See ORN.

ARP.

As in *carp*. Carp, harp, sharp, counterscarp.
As in *warp*. Warp. See ORP.

ARRH.

Catarrh. See AR.

ARSE.

See ARCE.

ARSH.

Harsh, marsh.

ART.

As in *art*. Heart, art, cart, dart, hart, mart, part, smart, tart, start, apart, depart, impart, dispart, counterpart.
As in *wart*. See ORT.

ARTH.

Swarth, forth, north.

ARVE.

Carve, starve.

AS.

As in *was*. Was, 'cos, poz.
As in *gas*. Gas. See ASS.
As in *has*. Has, as.

ASE.

As in *base*. See ACE.
As in *phrase*. See AZE.

ASH.

As in *ash*. Ash, cash, dash, clash, crash, flash, gash, gnash, hash, lash, plash, bash, pash, brash, rash, thrash, slash, trash, abash, sash, splash.
As in *wash*. Wash, bosh, squash, quash, swash.

ASK.

Ask, task, bask, cask, flask, mask, hask, casque.

ASM.

Chasm, spasm, miasm, enthusiasm, cataplasm, phantasm.

ASP.

Asp, clasp, rasp, gasp, grasp, hasp, wasp (?).

ASQUE.

Casque. See ASK.

ASS.

Ass, brass, class, grass, lass, mass, pass, alas, amass, cuirass, repass, surpass, morass, gas, alias.

AST.

Cast, last, blast, mast, past, vast, hast, fast, aghast, avast, forecast, overcast, outcast, repast, the preterites and participles of verbs in ASS.

ASTE.

Baste, chaste, haste, paste, taste, waste, distaste, waist, and the preterites and participles of verbs under ACE.

AT.

As in *at*. At, bat, cat, hat, fat, mat, pat, rat, sat, tat, vat, brat, chat, flat, lat, sprat, that, gnat.
As in *what*. See OT.

ATCH.

As in *catch*. Catch, match, hatch, latch, patch, scratch, smatch, snatch, dispatch, ratch, slatch, swatch, attach, detach, thatch.
As in *watch*. Watch. See OTCH.

ATE.

Bate, date, fate, gate, grate, hate, mate, pate, plate, prate, rate, sate, state, scate, slate, abate, belate, collate, create, debate, elate, dilate, estate, ingrate, innate, rebate, relate, sedate, translate, abdicate, abominate, abrogate, accelerate, accommodate, accumulate, accurate, adequate, affectionate, advocate, adulterate, aggravate, agitate, alienate, animate, annihilate, antedate, anticipate, antiquate, arbitrate, arrogate, articulate, assassinate, calculate, capitulate, captivate, celebrate, circulate, coagulate, commemorate, commiserate, communicate, compassionate, confederate, congratulate, congregate, consecrate, contaminate, corroborate, cultivate, candidate, co-operate, celibate, considerate, consulate, capacitate, debilitate, dedicate, degenerate, delegate, deliberate, denominate, depopulate, dislocate, deprecate, discriminate, derogate, dissipate, delicate, disconsolate, desolate, desperate, educate, effeminate, elevate, emulate, estimate, elaborate, equivocate, eradicate, evaporate, exaggerate, exasperate, expostulate, exterminate, extricate, facilitate, fortunate, generate, gratulate, hesitate, illiterate, illuminate, irritate, imitate, immoderate, impetrate, importunate, imprecate, inanimate, innovate, instigate, intemperate, intimate, intimidate, intoxicate, intricate, invalidate, inveterate, inviolate, legitimate, magistrate, meditate, mitigate, moderate, necessitate, nominate, obstinate, participate, passionate, penetrate, perpetrate, personate, potentate, precipitate, predestinate, predominate, premeditate, prevaricate, procrastinate, profligate, prognosticate, propagate, recriminate, regenerate, regulate, reiterate, reprobate, reverberate, ruminate, separate, sophisticate, stipulate, subjugate, subordinate, suffocate, terminate, titivate, tolerate, vindicate, violate, unfortunate, bait, strait, waite, await, great, tête-à-tête, eight, weight, straight.

Ate (from *eat*). Rhymes yet.

ATH.

As in *bath*. Bath, path, swath, wrath, hath, aftermath.

As in *rath*. See AITH.

ATHE.

Bathe, swathe, rathe, scathe.

AUB.

Daub, kebaub, Punjaub.

AUD.

Fraud, laud, applaud, defraud, broad, abroad, and the preterites and participles of verbs under Aw.

AUGH.

As in *laugh*. See AFF.
As in *usquebaugh*. See AW.

AUGHT.

As in *draught*. Draught, quaffed, etc.
As in *caught*. See AUT.

AUK.

See ALK.

AULM.

Haulm, shawm.

AULK.

Caulk. See ALK.

AULT.

See ALT.

AUN.

See AWN.

AUNCH.

See ANCH.

AUND.

Maund, preterites and participles of verbs in AWN.

AUNCE.

Askaunce, romance, glance, etc.

DICTIONARY OF RHYMES. 141

AUNT.

Aunt, daunt, gaunt, haunt, jaunt, taunt, vaunt, avaunt, shan't, can't.

AUR.

See ORE.

AUSE.

Cause, pause, clause, applause, gauze, because, the plurals of nouns and third persons singular of verbs in Aw.

AUST.

Holocaust. See OST.

AUT.

Taut, caught, ought, haught, sought, taught, fraught, distraught, nought.

AUZE.

See AUSE.

AVE.

Cave, brave, gave, grave, crave, lave, nave, knave, pave, rave, save, shave, slave, stave, wave, behave, deprave, engrave, outbrave, forgave, misgave, architrave. (*Have* has no rhyme.)

AW.

Craw, daw, law, chaw, claw, draw, flaw, gnaw, jaw, maw, paw, raw, saw, scraw, shaw, straw, thaw, withdraw, foresaw, usquebaugh.

AWD.

See AUD.

See ALK.

See ALL.

AWK.

AWL.

AWM.

Shawm. See AULM.

AWN.

Dawn, brawn, fawn, pawn, spawn, drawn, yawn, awn, withdrawn, aun, shaun, lawn, prawn.

AX.

Ax, tax, lax, pax, wax, relax, flax, knicknacks, the plurals of nouns and third persons singular of verbs in ACK.

AY.

Bray, clay, day, dray, tray, flay, fray, gay, hay, jay, lay, may, nay, pay, play, ray, say, way, pray, spray, slay, stay, stray, sway, tway, fay, affray, allay, array, astray, away, belay, bewray, betray, decay, defray, delay, disarray, display, dismay, essay, forelay, gainsay, inlay, relay, repay, roundelay, virelay, neigh, weigh, inveigh, shay, prey, they, convey, yea, obey, purvey, survey, disobey, gray, aye, denay.

AZE.

Craze, draze, blaze, gaze, glaze, raze, maze, amaze, graze, raise, praise, dispraise, phrase, paraphrase, and the nouns plural and third persons singular of the present tense of verbs in AY, EIGH, and EY.

E

E.
See EE.

CRE, CHRE, TRE.
Sepulchre, massacre, theatre. See ER.

EA.
As in *sea*. See EE.
As in *yea*. See AY.

EACE.
See EASE.

EACH.
Beach, breach, bleach, each, peach, preach, teach, impeach, beech, leech, speech, beseech.

EAD.
As in *bread*. See ED.
As in *read*. See EED.

EAF.
As in *sheaf*. See IEF.
As in *deaf*. See EF.

EAGUE.
League, Teague, intrigue, fatigue.

EAK.
As in *beak*. Beak, speak, bleak, creak, freak, leak, peak, sneak, squeak, streak, weak, tweak, wreak, be-

speak, cheek, leek, eke, creek, meek, reek, seek, sleek, pique, bezique, clique, critique, antique, oblique, week, shriek.

As in *break*. See AKE.

EAL.

Deal, heal, reveal, meal, peal, seal, steal, teal, veal, weal, squeal, leal, zeal, repeal, conceal, congeal, repeal, anneal, appeal, wheal, eel, heel, feel, keel, kneel, peel, reel, steal, wheel. (Real is a dissyllable, and therefore does not count here.)

EALD.

Weald. See IELD.

EALM.

See ELM.

EALTH.

Health, wealth, stealth, commonwealth.

EAM.

Bream, cream, gleam, seam, scream, stream, team, beam, dream, enseam, scheme, theme, blaspheme, extreme, supreme, deem, teem, beseem, misdeem, esteem, disesteem, redeem, seem, beteem.

EAMT.

Dreamt, exempt, attempt, empt.

EAN.

Bean, clean, dean, glean, lean, mean, wean, yean, demean, unclean, convene, demesne, intervene, mien, hyen, machine, keen, screen, seen, skean, green, spleen, between, careen, teen, foreseen, serene, obscene, terrene, queen, spleen, etc.

EANS.

Means, rhymes plural of nouns, and third persons singular present of verbs, in EAN, EEN, ENE.

EANSE.

Cleanse, plural of nouns, and third person singular present of verbs, in EN.

EANT.

See ENT.

EAP.

See EEP.

EAR.

See EER and AIR.

EARCH.

Search, research. See URCH.

EARD.

As in *heard*. See URD.

As in *beard*. Beard, feared, revered, weird, preterites and participles of verbs in EAR, ERE, etc.

EARL.

Earl, pearl, girl, curl, churl, whirl, purl, furl, thirl, twirl.

EARN.

See ERN.

EARSE.

See ERSE.

EART.

See ART.

EARTH.

Earth, dearth, birth, mirth, worth, Perth, berth.

EASE.

As in *cease.* Cease, lease, release, grease, decease, decrease, increase, release, surcease, peace, piece, niece, fleece, geese, frontispiece, apiece, etc.

As in *disease.* See EEZE.

EAST.

East, feast, least, beast, priest, the preterites and participles of verbs in EASE, as in *cease.*

EAT.

As in *bleat.* Bleat, eat, feat, heat, meat, neat, seat, effete, treat, wheat, beat, cheat, defeat, estreat, escheat, entreat, retreat, obsolete, replete, concrete, complete, feet, fleet, greet, meet, sheet, sleet, street, sweet, discreet.

As in *great.* See ATE.
As in *threat.* See ET.

EATH.

As in *breath*. Breath, death, saith, Elizabeth, etc., and antiquated third person singular present, accented on the antepenult (e. g., "encountereth").

As in *heath*. Heath, sheath, teeth, wreath, beneath.

EATHE.

Breathe, sheathe, wreathe, inwreathe, bequeathe, seethe.

EAU.

See O.

EAVE.

Cleave, heave, interweave, leave, weave, bereave, inweave, receive, conceive, deceive, perceive, eve, grieve, sleeve, thieve, aggrieve, achieve, believe, disbelieve, relieve, reprieve, retrieve.

EB, and EBB.

Web, neb, ebb, bleb.

ECK, and EC.

Beck, peck, neck, check, fleck, deck, speck, wreck, hypothec, spec, geck.

EKS.

I'fecks, third person singular of verbs and plural of nouns in ECK.

ECT.

Sect, affect, correct, incorrect, collect, deject, detect, direct, disrespect, disaffect, dissect, effect, elect, eject, erect, expect, indirect, infect, inspect, neglect, object, project, protect, recollect, reflect, reject, respect, select, subject, suspect, architect, circumspect, direct, intellect, the preterites and participles of verbs in ECK, etc.

ED.

Bed, bled, fed, fled, bred, Ted, red, shred, shed, sped, wed, abed, imbred, misled, said, bread, dread, dead, head, lead, read, spread, thread, tread, behead, o'erspread, and the preterites and participles of verbs, which, when the "éd" (pronounced) is added, have the accent on the antepenultimate (e. g., vanishéd; but see Chapter VIII).

EDE.

See EED.

EDGE.

Edge, wedge, fledge, hedge, ledge, pledge, sedge, allege, kedge, privilege, sacrilege, sortilege.

EE.

Bee, free, glee, knee, see, three, thee, tree, agree, decree, degree, disagree, flee, foresee, o'ersee, pedigree, he, me, we, she, be, jubilee, lee, ne, sea, plea, flea, tea, key, cap-à-pie, gree, dree, calipee.

EECE.

See EASE.

EECH.
See EACH.

EED.
Creed, deed, indeed, bleed, breed, feed, heed, meed, need, reed, speed, seed, steed, weed, proceed, succeed, exceed, knead, read, intercede, precede, recede, concede, impede, supersede, glede, rede, bead, lead, mead, read, plead, etc.

EEF.
See IEF.

EEK.
See EAK.

EEL.
See EAL.

EEM.
See EAM.

EEN.
See EAN.

EEP.
Creep, deep, sleep, keep, peep, sheep, steep, sweep, weep, asleep, cheap, heap, neap.

EER.
As in *beer*. Beer, deer, fleer, geer, jeer, peer, mere, leer, sheer, steer, sneer, cheer, veer, pickeer, domineer, cannoneer, compeer, engineer, mutineer, pioneer, privateer, charioteer, chanticleer, career, mountaineer, fere, here, sphere, adhere, cohere, interfere, persevere, revere, austere, severe, sincere,

hemisphere, etc.; ear, clear, dear, fear, near, sear, hear, pier, bier, tier, smear, spear, tear, rear, year, appear, besmear, bandolier, disappear, endear, auctioneer.

As in *e'er*. See ARE.

EESE.
See EEZE.

EET.
See EAT.

EETH.
See EATH.

EETHE.
See EATHE.

EEVE.
See EAVE.

EEVES.
. Beaves rhymes plural of nouns and third person singular present of verbs in EEVE, IEVE, etc.

EEZE.
Breeze, freeze, wheeze, sneeze, squeeze, and the plurals of nouns and third persons singular present tense of verbs in EE, cheese, leese, these, ease, appease, disease, displease, tease, seize, and the plurals of nouns in EA, EE, etc.

EF.
Clef, nef, semibref, kef, deaf.

EFT.
Cleft, left, theft, weft, bereft.

EG and EGG.
Egg, leg, beg, peg, Meg, keg, Winnepeg.

EGM.
See EM.

EGN.
Thegn. See AIN.

EH.
Eh? See AY.

EIGH.
See AY.

EIGHT.
See ATE and ITE.

EIGN.
See AIN.

EIL.
See EEL and AIL.

EIN.
See AIN.

EINT.
See AINT.

EIR.
See ARE.

EIRD.
Weird. See EARD.

EIT.
See EAT.

EIVE.
See EAVE.

EIZE.
See EEZE.

EKE.
See EAK.

EL, and ELL.
Ell, dwell, fell, hell, knell, quell, sell, bell, cell, mell, dispel, foretell, excel, compel, befell, yell, well, tell, swell, spell, smell, shell, parallel, sentinel, infidel, citadel, refel, repel, rebel, impel, expel, asphodel, petronel, calomel, muscatel.

ELD.
Held, geld, withheld, upheld, beheld, eld, etc., the preterites and participles of verbs in EL, ELL.

ELF.
Elf, delf, pelf, self, shelf, himself, Guelf, Guelph.

ELK.
Elk, kelk, whelk.

ELM.
Elm, helm, realm, whelm, overwhelm.

ELP.
Help, whelp, kelp, yelp.

ELT.
Belt, gelt, melt, felt, welt, smelt, pelt, dwelt, dealt.

ELVE.
Delve, helve, shelve, twelve.

ELVES.
Elves, themselves, the plurals of nouns and third persons singular of verbs in ELVE.

EM.
Gem, hem, stem, them, diadem, stratagem, anadem, kemb, phlegm, condemn, contemn, parapegm, apothegm.

EME.
See EAM.

EMN.
See EM.

EMPT.
Tempt, exempt, attempt, contempt, dreamt.

EN.
Den, hen, fen, ken, men, pen, ten, then, when, wren, denizen. Hyen rhymes EEN.

ENCE.
Fence, hence, pence, thence, whence, defence, expense, offence, pretence, commence, abstinence, circumference, conference, confidence, consequence, continence,

benevolence, concupiscence, difference, diffidence, diligence, eloquence, eminence, evidence, excellence, impenitence, impertinence, impotence, impudence, improvidence, incontinence, indifference, indigence, indolence, inference, intelligence, innocence, magnificence, munificence, negligence, omnipotence, penitence, preference, providence, recompense, reference, residence, reverence, vehemence, violence, sense, dense, cense, condense, immense, intense, propense, dispense, suspense, prepense, incense, frankincense.

ENCH.

Bench, drench, retrench, quench, clench, stench, tench, trench, wench, wrench, intrench, blench.

END.

Bend, mend, blend, end, fend, lend, rend, send, spend, tend, vend, amend, attend, ascend, commend, contend, defend, depend, descend, distend, expend, extend, forefend, impend, misspend, obtend, offend, portend, pretend, protend, suspend, transcend, unbend, apprehend, comprehend, condescend, discommend, recommend, reprehend, dividend, reverend, friend, befriend, and the preterites and participles of verbs in EN, etc.

ENDS.

Amends, the plurals of nouns and third persons singular present tense of verbs in END.

ENE.

See EAN.

DICTIONARY OF RHYMES. 155

ENGE.

Avenge, revenge, no rhyme.

ENGTH.

Length, strength.

ENS.

Lens, plural of nouns and third person singular present of verbs in EN.

ENT.

Bent, lent, rent, pent, scent, sent, shent, spent, tent, vent, went, blent, cement, brent, hent, absent, meant, ascent, assent, attent, augment, cement, content, consent, descent, dissent, event, extent, foment, frequent, indent, intent, invent, lament, misspent, o'erspent, present, prevent, relent, repent, resent, ostent, ferment, outwent, underwent, discontent, unbent, circumvent, represent, abstinent, accident, accomplishment, admonishment, acknowledgment, aliment, arbitrament, argument, banishment, battlement, blandishment, astonishment, armipotent, bellipotent, benevolent, chastisement, competent, complement, compliment, confident, continent, corpulent, detriment, different, diligent, disparagement, document, element, eloquent, eminent, equivalent, establishment, evident, excellent, excrement, exigent, experiment, firmament, fraudulent, government, embellishment, imminent, impenitent, impertinent, implement, impotent, imprisonment, improvident, impudent, incident, incompetent, incontinent, indifferent, indigent, innocent, insolent, instrument, irreverent, languishment, ligament, lineament, magnificent, management, medicament, malecontent, monument, negligent, nourishment, nutriment, occident, omnipotent, opulent, ornament, parliament, penitent, permanent, pertinent, president, precedent, prevalent, provident, punishment, ravishment, regiment, resident, redolent, rudiment, sacrament, sediment, sentiment, settlement, subsequent, supplement, intelligent, tenement, temperament, testament, tournament, turbulent, vehement, violent, virulent, reverent.

ENTS.

Accoutrements, the plurals of nouns and third persons singular present tense of verbs in ENT.

EP.

Step, nep, skep, rep, demirep.

EPT.

Accept, adept, except, intercept, crept, sept, slept, wept, kept.

ER, and ERR.

Her, sir, fir, burr, cur, err, aver, defer, infer, deter, inter, refer, transfer, confer, prefer, whirr, administer, wagoner, islander, arbiter, character, villager, cottager, dowager, forager, pillager, voyager, massacre, gardener, slanderer, flatterer, idolater, provender, theatre, amphitheatre, foreigner, lavender, messenger, passenger, sorcerer, interpreter, officer, mariner, harbinger, minister, register, canister, chorister, sophister, presbyter, lawgiver, philosopher, astrologer, loiterer, prisoner, grasshopper, astronomer, sepulchre, thunderer, traveler, murderer, usurer, myrrh, purr, stir, slur, fur, bur, spur, concur, demur, incur, skirr.

ERCH.
See EARCH.

ERCE.
See ERSE.

IERCE.
See ERSE.

ERD.
See EARD.

ERE.
See EER.

ERF.
Serf, turf, surf, scurf.

ERGE.
Verge, absterge, emerge, immerge, dirge, urge, purge, surge.

ERGUE.
Exergue, burgh.

ERM.
Term, firm, worm, affirm, confirm infirm, chirm, turm.

ERN.
Fern, stern, discern, hern, concern, learn, earn, yearn, quern, dern, burn, eterne, turn.

ERNE.
Eterne. See ERN.

ERP.
Discerp. See IRP.

ERSE.
Verse, absterse, adverse, averse, converse, terse, disperse, immerse, perverse, reverse, asperse, intersperse, universe, amerce, coerce, hearse, purse, curse, nurse, etc., accurse, disburse, imburse, reimburse, worse.

ERT.
Wert, advert, assert, avert, concert, convert, controvert, desert, divert, exert, expert, insert, invert, pervert, subvert, shirt, dirt, sqirt, flirt, blurt, hurt, spurt.

ERTH.
Berth, birth, mirth, earth, worth, dearth, girth, perth.

ERVE.
Serve, nerve, swerve, preserve, deserve, conserve, observe, reserve, disserve, subserve, curve.

ES, ESS, or ESSE.
Yes, bless, dress, cess, chess, guess, less, mess, press, stress, acquiesce, access, address, assess, compress, confess, caress, depress, digress, dispossess, distress, excess, express, impress, oppress, possess, profess, recess, repress, redress, success, transgress, adultress,

DICTIONARY OF RHYMES. 159

bashfulness, bitterness, cheerfulness, comfortless, comeliness, dizziness, diocess, drowsiness, eagerness, easiness, ambassadress, emptiness, evenness, fatherless, filthiness, foolishness, forgetfulness, forwardness, frowardness, fruitfulness, fulsomeness, giddiness, greediness, gentleness, governess, happiness, haughtiness, heaviness, idleness, heinousness, hoariness, hollowness, holiness, lasciviousness, lawfulness, laziness, littleness, liveliness, loftiness, lioness, lowliness, manliness, masterless, mightiness, motherless, motionless, nakedness, neediness, noisomeness, numberless, patroness, peevishness, perfidiousness, pitiless, poetess, prophetess, ransomless, readiness, righteousness, shepherdess, sorceress, sordidness, spiritless, sprightliness, stubbornness, sturdiness, surliness, steadiness, tenderness, thoughtfulness, ugliness, uneasiness, unhappiness, votaress, usefulness, wakefulness, wantonness, weaponless, wariness, willingness, willfulness, weariness, wickedness, wilderness, wretchedness, drunkenness, childishness, duresse, cesse.

ESE.

See EEZE.

ESH.

Flesh, fresh, refresh, thresh, afresh, nesh, mesh.

ESK, and ESQUE.

Desk, grotesque, burlesque, arabesque, picturesque, moresque.

EST.

Best, chest, crest, guest, jest, nest, pest, quest, rest, test, vest, lest, west, arrest, attest, bequest, contest, detest, digest, divest, invest, palimpsest, alcahest, infest, molest, obtest, protest, request, suggest, unrest, interest, manifest, breast, abreast, and the preterites and participles of verbs in Ess.

ET, and ETTE.

Bet, get, jet, fret, let, met, net, set, wet, whet, yet, debt, abet, beget, beset, forget, regret, alphabet, amulet, anchoret, cabinet, epithet, parapet, rivulet, violet, coronet, parroquet, basinet, wagonette, cadet, epaulette, piquette, sweat, threat, rosette, silhouette.

ETCH.

Fetch, stretch, wretch, sketch.

ETE.

See Eat.

ETH.

See Eath.

EVE.

See Eave.

EUCE.

See Use.

EUD.

See Ude.

EUM.

See Ume.

EUR.

Amateur, connoisseur, bon-viveur.

EW.

Blew, chew, dew, brew, drew, flew, few, grew, new, coo, woo, shoe, too, who, do, blue, stew, knew, hew, Jew, mew, view, threw, yew, crew, slew, anew, askew, bedew, eschew, renew, review, withdrew, screw, interview, emmew, clue, due, cue, glue, hue, rue, sue, true, accrue, ensue, endue, imbue, imbrue, pursue, subdue, adieu, purlieu, perdue, residue, ormolu, avenue, revenue, retinue, through, pooh, you. (News takes plural of nouns and third person singular present of verbs of this class.)

EWD.

See UDE.

EWN.

See UNE.

EX.

Sex, vex, annex, convex, complex, perplex, circumflex, and the plurals of nouns and third persons singular of verbs in EC, ECK.

EXT.

Next, pretext, and the preterites and participles of verbs in EX.

EY.

As in *prey*. See AY.
As in *key*. See EE.

EYNE.

Eyne rhymes INE.

I.

See IE.

IB.

Bib, crib, squib, drib, glib, nib, rib.

IBE.

Bribe, tribe, kibe, scribe, ascribe, describe, superscribe, prescribe, proscribe, subscribe, transcribe, inscribe, imbibe, diatribe.

IC.

See ICK.

ICE.

Ice, dice, mice, nice, price, rice, spice, slice, thrice, trice, splice, advice, entice, vice, device, concise, precise, paradise, sacrifice.

ICHE and ICH.

See ITCH.

ICK.

Brick, sick, chick, kick, lick, nick, pick, quick, stick, thick, trick, arithmetic, choleric, catholic, heretic, rhetoric, splenetic, lunatic, politic.

ICT.

Strict, addict, afflict, convict, inflict, contradict, Pict. The preterites and participles of verbs in ICK.

ID.

Bid, chid, hid, kid, lid, slid, rid, bestrid, pyramid, forbid, quid, squid, katydid.

IDE.

Bide, chide, hide, gride, glide, pride, ride, slide, side, nide, stride, tide, wide, bride, abide, guide, aside, astride, beside, bestride, betide, confide, decide, deride, divide, preside, provide, subside, misguide, subdivide, the preterites and participles of verbs in IE, IGH, and Y.

IDES.

Ides, besides, the plurals of nouns and third persons singular of verbs in IDE.

IDGE.

Bridge, ridge, midge, fidge, abridge.

IDST.

Midst, amidst, didst, the second persons singular of the present tense of verbs in ID.

IE, or Y.

By, buy, cry, die, dry, eye, fly, fry, fie, hie, lie, pie, alibi, alkali, ply, pry, rye, shy, sly, spy, sky, sty, tie, try, vie, why, ally, apply, awry, bely, comply, decry, defy, descry, deny, imply, espy, outvie, outfly, rely, reply, supply, untie, amplify, beautify, certify, crucify, deify, dignify, edify, falsify, fortify, gratify, glorify, indemnify, justify, magnify, modify, mollify, mortify, pacify, petrify, purify, putrify, qualify, ratify, rectify, sanctify, satisfy, scarify, signify, specify, stupefy, terrify, testify, verify, vilify, vitrify, vivify, prophesy, high, nigh, sigh, thigh. Such words as *lunacy, polygamy, tyranny*, can not well be used, as it is difficult to get the *y* sound without over-accentuating it.

IECE.
See EASE.

IED.
Pied, side, sighed, rhymes with preterites and participles of verbs in Y or IE.

IEF.
Grief, chief, fief, thief, brief, belief, relief, reef, beef, leaf, sheaf.

IEGE.
Liege, siege, assiege, besiege.

IELD.
Field, yield, shield, wield, afield, weald, and the preterites and participles of verbs in EAL.

IEN.
See EEN.

IEND.
As in *fiend*. Rhymes preterites and participles of verbs in EAN, EEN.

As in *friend*. Rhymes END.

IER.
See EER.

IERCE.
Fierce, pierce, tierce.

IEST.
Priest rhymes EAST. *Diest*, second person singular present, at times pronounced as a monosyllable, rhymes *spiced*, etc.

IEVE.
As in *sieve*. See IVE.
As in *grieve*. See EAVE.

IEU.
See EW.

IEZE.
Frieze. See EEZE.

IF, IFF.
If, skiff, stiff, whiff, cliff, sniff, tiff, hieroglyph.

IFE.
Rife, fife, knife, wife, strife, life.

IFT.
Gift, drift, shift, lift, rift, sift, thrift, adrift, and the preterites and participles of verbs in IFF.

IG.

Big, dig, gig, fig, pig, rig, sprig, twig, swig, grig, Whig, wig, jig, prig.

IGE.
Oblige, no rhyme.

IGH.
See IE.

IGHT.
See ITE.

IGM.
See IME.

IGN.
See INE.

IGUE.
See EAGUE.

IKE.
Dike, like, pike, spike, strike, alike, dislike, shrike, glike.

IL, ILL.
Bill, chill, fill, drill, gill, hill, ill, kill, mill, pill, quill, rill, shrill, fill, skill, spill, still, swill, thrill, till, trill, will, distill, fulfill, instill, codicil, daffodil.

ILCH.
Filch, milch.

ILD.
As in *child*. Rhymes mild, wild, guild, etc., the preterites and participles of verbs of one syllable in

ILE, or of more syllables, provided the accent be on the last.

As in *gild*. Rhymes build, rebuild, etc., and the preterites and participles of verbs in ILL.

ILE.

Bile, chyle, file, guile, isle, mile, pile, smile, stile, style, tile, vile, while, awhile, compile, revile, defile, exile, erewhile, reconcile, beguile, aisle. (There is also the *eel* sound, as in imported words like bastile, pastile, rhyming with EAL.)

ILGE.

Bilge, no rhyme.

ILK.

Milk, silk, bilk, whilk.

ILN.

Kiln, no rhyme.

ILT.

Gilt, jilt, built, quilt, hilt, guilt, spilt, stilt, tilt, milt.

ILTH.

Filth, tilth, spilth.

IM.

Brim, dim, grim, him, rim, skim, slim, trim, whim, prim, limb, hymn, limn.

IMB.
As in *limb*. See IM.
As in *climb*. See IME.

IME.
Chime, time, grime, climb, clime, crime, prime, mime, rhyme, slime, thyme, lime, sublime, paradigm.

IMES.
Betimes, sometimes. Rhymes the plurals of nouns and third persons singular present tense of verbs in IME.

IMN.
See IM.

IMP.
Imp, limp, pimp, gimp, jimp.

IMPSE.
Glimpse. Rhymes the plurals of nouns and third persons singular present tense of verbs in IMP.

IN, INN.
Bin, chin, din, fin, gin, grin, in, inn, kin, pin, shin, sin, spin, skin, linn, thin, twin, tin, win, within, javelin, begin, whin, baldachin, cannikin, discipline.

INC.
See INK.

INCE.
Mince, prince, since, quince, rinse, wince, convince, evince.

INCH.

Clinch, finch, winch, pinch, inch.

INCT.

Instinct, distinct, extinct, precinct, succinct, tinct, etc., and the preterites and participles of certain verbs in INK, as linked, pinked, etc.

IND.

As in *bind*. Find, mind, blind, kind, grind, rind, wind, behind, unkind, remind, etc., and the preterites and participles of verbs in INE, IGN, etc.

As in *rescind*. Preterites and participles of verbs in IN.

INE.

As in *dine*. Brine, mine, chine, fine, line, nine, pine, shine, shrine, kine, thine, trine, twine, vine, wine, whine, combine, confine, decline, define, incline, enshrine, entwine, opine, recline, refine, repine, superfine, interline, countermine, undermine, supine, concubine, porcupine, Rhine, divine, sign, assign, consign, design, eyne, condign, indign.

As in *discipline*. See IN.

ING.

Bring, sing, cling, fling, king, ring, sling, spring, sting, string, ging, swing, wing, wring, thing, etc., and the participles of the present tense in ING, with the accent on the antepenultimate, as *recovering*.

INGE.

Cringe, fringe, hinge, singe, springe, swinge, tinge, twinge, infringe.

INK and INQUE.

Ink, think, wink, drink, blink, brink, chink, clink, link, pink, shrink, sink, slink, stink, bethink, forethink, skink, swink, zinc, cinque, appropinque.

INSE.

Rinse. See INCE.

INT.

Dint, mint, hint, flint, lint, print, squint, asquint, imprint, sprint, quint.

INTH.

Plinth, hyacinth, labyrinth.

INX.

Minx, sphinx, methinks, jinks, plural of nouns and third person singular present of verb in INK.

IP.

Chip, lip, hip, clip, dip, drip, lip, nip, sip, rip, scrip, ship, skip, slip, snip, strip, tip, trip, whip, equip, eldership, fellowship, workmanship, rivalship, and all words in SHIP with the accent on the antepenultimate.

IPE.

Gripe, pipe, ripe, snipe, type, stripe, wipe, archetype, prototype.

DICTIONARY OF RHYMES.   171

IPSE.
Eclipse. Rhymes the plurals of nouns and third persons singular present tense in IP.

IQUE.
See EAK.

IR.
See UR.

IRCH.
See URCH.

IRD.
See URD.

IRE.
Fire, dire, hire, ire, lyre, mire, quire, sire, spire, squire, wire, tire, attire, acquire, admire, aspire, conspire, desire, inquire, entire, expire, inspire, require, retire, transpire, pyre, gipsire, gire.

IRGE.
See ERGE.

IRK.
Dirk, firk, kirk, stirk, quirk, shirk, work, burke, murk.

IRL.
See EARL.

IRM.
See ERM.

IRR.
See ER.

IRP.
See URP.

IRST.
See URST.

IRT.
See URT.

IRTH.
See ERTH.

IS.
Pronounced like *iz*. Is, his, whiz.

ISS.
Bliss, miss, hiss, kiss, this, abyss, amiss, submiss, dismiss, remiss, wis, Dis, spiss.

ISC.
Disc, whisk, risk. See ISK.

ISE.
See ICE and IZE.

ISH.
Dish, fish, wish, cuish, pish, squish.

ISK.
Brisk, frisk, disc, risk, whisk, basilisk, tamarisk.

ISM.
Chrism, solecism, anachronism, abysm, schism, syllogism, witticism, criticism, organism, heroism, prism, egotism, cataclysm.

ISP.
Crisp, wisp, lisp.

IST.
Fist, list, mist, twist, wrist, assist, consist, desist, exist, insist, persist, resist, subsist, alchemist, amethyst, anatomist, antagonist, annalist, evangelist, eucharist, exorcist, herbalist, humorist, oculist, organist, satirist, etc., and the preterites and participles of verbs in Iss, etc.

IT.
Bit, Cit, hit, fit, grit, flit, knit, pit, quit, sit, split, twit, wit, chit, whit, writ, admit, acquit, commit, emit, omit, outwit, permit, remit, submit, transmit, refit, benefit, perquisite.

ITCH.
Ditch, pitch, rich, which, flitch, itch, stitch, switch, twitch, witch, bewitch, niche, enrich, fitch.

ITE, and IGHT.
Bite, cite, kite, blite, mite, quite, rite, smite, spite, trite, white, write, contrite, disunite, despite, indite, excite, incite, invite, polite, requite, recite, unite, reunite, aconite, appetite, parasite, proselyte, expedite, blight, benight, bright, fight, flight, fright, height, light, knight, night, might, wight, plight, right, tight, slight, sight, spright, wight, affright, alight, aright, foresight, delight, despite, unsight, upright, benight, bedight, oversight, height, accite, pight.

ITH.
Pith, smith, frith, sith. (*With* has strictly no rhyme.)

ITHE.
Hithe, blithe, tithe, scythe, writhe, lithe.

ITS.
Quits rhymes plural of nouns and third person singular present of verbs in IT.

IVE.
As in *five*. Rhymes dive, alive, gyve, hive, drive, rive, shrive, strive, thrive, arrive, connive, contrive, deprive, derive, revive, survive.

As in *give*. Rhymes live, sieve, fugitive, positive, sensitive, etc.

IX.
Fix, six, mix, nix, affix, infix, prefix, transfix, intermix, crucifix, etc., and the plurals of nouns and third persons singular of verbs in ICK.

IXT.
Betwixt. Rhymes the preterites and participles of verbs in Ix.

ISE, and IZE.
Prize, wise, rise, size, guise, disguise, advise, authorise, canonise, agonise, chastise, civilise, comprise, criticise, despise, devise, enterprise, excise, exercise, idolise, immortalise, premise, revise, signalise, solemnise, surprise, surmise, suffice, sacrifice, sympathise, tyrannise, and the plurals of nouns and third persons singular present tense of verbs in IE or Y.

O

O.

Mo', calico, bo, portico, go, ago, undergo, ho, though, woe, adagio, seraglio, owe, beau, crow, lo, no, fro', so, snow, show, slow, overthrow, overflow, foreshow, outgrow, dough, foreknow, forego, undergo, below, bestow, tho', hoe, ho, ago, strow, slow, mistletoe, sloe, toe, Co, foe, doe, roe, oh, stow, bow, flow, glow, grow, know, low, mow, sew.

OACH.

Broach, coach, poach, abroach, approach, encroach, reproach, loach.

OAD.

See ODE.

OAF.

Oaf, loaf.

OAK.

See OKE.

OAL.

See OLE.

OAM.

See OME.

OAN.

See ONE.

OAP.

See OPE.

OAR.
See ORE.

OARD.
See ORD.

OAST.
See OST.

OAT.
See OTE.

OATH.
See OTH.

OAVES.
Loaves, groves, roves, cloves, etc.

OAX.
Hoax, coax, rhyme plural of nouns and third person singular present of verbs in OKE.

OB.
Cob, fob, bob, lob, hob, nob, mob, knob, sob, rob, throb, cabob, swab, squab.

OBE.
Globe, lobe, probe, robe, conglobe.

OCE.
See OSE.

OCH.
See OCK.

OCHE.

Caroche, gauche.

OCK.

Block, lock, cock, clock, crock, dock, frock, flock, knock, mock, rock, shock, stock, sock, brock, hough, loch, epoch.

OCT.

Concoct rhymes the preterites and participles of verbs in OCK.

OD.

Cod, clod, God, rod, sod, trod, nod, plod, odd, shod, quod, pod, wad, quad, odd, hod, tod.

ODE.

Bode, ode, code, mode, rode, abode, corrode, explode, forebode, commode, incommode, episode, à-la-mode, road, toad, goad, load, etc., and the preterites and participles of verbs in OW, OWE.

ODGE.

Dodge, lodge, Hodge, podge, bodge.

OE.

As in *shoe*. See OO.
As in *toe*. See O.

OFF.

Doff, off, scoff, cough.

OFT.

Oft, croft, soft, aloft, and the preterites and participles of verbs in OFF.

OG.

Hog, bog, cog, dog, clog, fog, frog, log, jog, agog, Gog, prog, quog, shog, tog, pollywog, dialogue, epilogue, synagogue, catalogue, pedagogue, Quogue.

OGE.

Gamboge, rouge.

OGUE.

As in *rogue*. Rhymes vogue, prorogue, collogue, disembogue.
As in *catalogue*. See OG.

OH.

See O.

OICE.

Choice, voice, rejoice.

OID.

Void, avoid, devoid, asteroid, alkaloid, varioloid, and the preterites and participles of verbs in OY.

OIF.

Coif, no rhyme.

OIGN.

See OIN.

OIL.

Oil, boil, coil, moil, soil, spoil, toil, despoil, embroil, recoil, turmoil, disembroil.

OIN.

Coin, join, subjoin, groin, loin, adjoin, conjoin, disjoin, enjoin, foin, proin, purloin, rejoin, coign.

OINT.

Oint, joint, point, disjoint, anoint, appoint, aroint, disappoint, counterpoint.

OIR.

As in *choir*. See IRE, but the foreign sound, as in *devoir, reservoir*, is nearer AR, but must not be so rhymed. *Coir* is a dissyllable.

OISE.

Poise, noise, counterpoise, equipoise, etc., and the plurals of nouns and third persons singular present tense of verbs in OY.

OIST.

Hoist, moist, foist, the preterites and participles of verbs in OICE.

OIT.

Doit, exploit, adroit, quoit, etc.

OKE.

Broke, choke, smoke, spoke, stroke, yoke, bespoke, invoke, provoke, revoke, cloak, oak, soak, joke, moke, coke, equivoque.

OL.

Alcohol, loll, doll, extol, capitol, Moll, Poll.

OLD.

Old, bold, cold, gold, hold, mold, scold, sold, told, behold, enfold, unfold, uphold, withhold, foretold, manifold, marigold, preterites and participles of verbs in OLL, OWL, OLE, and OAL.

OLE.

Bole, dole, jole, hole, mole, pole, sole, stole, whole, shoal, cajole, girandole, condole, parole, patrole, pistole, console, aureole, vole, coal, foal, goal, bowl, roll, scroll, toll, troll, droll, poll, control, enrol, soul.

OLL.

As in *loll*. Rhymes OL.
As in *droll*. See OLE.

OLN.

Stol'n, swoln.

OLP.

Holp, golpe.

OLT.

Bolt, colt, jolt, holt, dolt, revolt, thunderbolt, moult.

OLVE.

Solve, absolve, resolve, convolve, involve, devolve, dissolve, revolve.

OM.

Tom, from. But for *whom*, see OOM.

OMB.

As in *tomb*. See OOM.
As in *comb*. See OME, clomb.
As in *bomb*. See UM. *Rhomb* has no rhyme.

OME.

Dome, home, mome, foam, roam, loam.

OMP.

Pomp, swamp, romp.

OMPT.

Prompt, preterite and participle of romp.

ON.

As in *don*. Rhymes on, con, upon, anon, shone.
As in *won*. See UN.

ONCE.

As in *sconce*. See ONSE.
As in *once*. See UNCE.

ONCH.

Conch, jonque.

OND.

Pond, bond, fond, beyond, abscond, correspond, blonde, despond, diamond, vagabond, and the preterites and participles of verbs in ON.

ONE.

As in *bone*. Prone, drone, throne, alone, stone, tone, lone, zone, atone, enthrone, dethrone, postpone, grown, flown, disown, thrown, sown, own, loan, shown, overthrown, groan, blown, moan, known, cone, loan.
As in *done*. See UN.
As in *gone*. See AWN.
As in *shone*. See ON.

ONG.

As in *long*. Prong, song, thong, strong, throng, wrong, along, belong, prolong.
As in *among*. See UNG.

ONGE.

See UNGE.

ONGUE.

See UNG.

ONK.

As in *monk*. See UNK.
As in *conk*. Rhymes jonque.

ONSE.

Response, sconce, ensconce.

ONT.

As in *font*. Rhymes want.
As in *front*. See UNT. (The abbreviated negatives, won't, don't, rhyme together.)

OO.

See EW.

OOCH.

See OACH.

OOD.

As in *brood*. See UDE.
As in *wood*. Rhymes good, hood, stood, withstood, understood, could, would, brotherhood, livelihood, likelihood, neighborhood, widowhood.
As in *blood*. See UD.

OOF.

Hoof, proof, roof, woof, aloof, disproof, reproof, behoof.

OOH.

See EW.

OOK.

Book, brook, cook, crook, hook, look, rook, shook, took, mistook, undertook, forsook, stook, betook, caoutchouc.

OOL.

Cool, fool, pool, school, stool, tool, befool, spool, buhl, pule, rule.

OOM.

Gloom, groom, loom, room, spoom, bloom, boom, doom, tomb, entomb, whom, womb, plume, spume, fume, consume, assume, presume, resume, perfume, rheum.

OON.

See UNE.

OOP.

Loop, poop, scoop, stoop, troop, droop, whoop, coop, hoop, soup, group, dupe.

OOR.

As in *boor*. Rhymes poor, moor, tour, amour, paramour, contour, pure, sure, your.

As in *door*. See ORE.

OOSE.

See USE.

OOT.

As in *root*. See UTE.

As in *foot*. Rhymes put. (It is difficult to say whether *soot* should rhyme *root* or *but*, the pronunciation so varies.)

OOTH.

As in *booth*. Rhymes smooth, soothe.
As in *tooth*. Rhymes youth, uncouth, truth.

OOVE.

See OVE.

OOZE.

Ooze, noose, whose, choose, lose, use, abuse, the plurals of nouns and third persons singular present tense of verbs in EW, UE.

OP.

Chop, hop, drop, crop, fop, top, pop, prop, flop, shop, slop, sop, stop, swop, underprop.

OPE.

Hope, cope, mope, grope, pope, rope, scope, slope, trope, aslope, elope, interlope, telescope, heliotrope, horoscope, antelope, etc., and ope, contracted in poetry for open.

OPT.

Adopt rhymes with the preterites and participles of verbs in OP, etc.

OQUE.

See OKE.

OR.

Or, for, creditor, counsellor, competitor, emperor, ancestor, ambassador, progenitor, conspirator, conqueror, governor, abhor, metaphor, bachelor, senator, etc., and every word in OR having the accent on the last, or last syllable but two, pour, bore, tore, boar, hoar, war, corps, tor.

ORB.
Orb, sorb, corb.

ORCE.
See ORSE.

ORCH.
Scorch, torch, porch.

ORD and ORDE.
As in *cord*. Rhymes lord, record, accord, abhorr'd, hoard, horde, board, aboard, ford, afford, sword, and the preterites and participles of verbs in OAR, ORE.
As in *word*. See URD.

ORE.
Bore, core, gore, lore, more, ore, pore, score, shore, snore, sore, store, swore, tore, wore, adore, afore, ashore, deplore, explore, implore, restore, forebore, foreswore, heretofore, hellebore, sycamore, albicore, boar, oar, roar, soar, four, door, floor, o'er, orator, senator, abhor, corps, encore, Bucentaur.

ORGE.
George, gorge, disgorge, regorge, forge.

ORK.
Ork, cork, fork, stork, pork, York.

ORLD.
World, rhymes with the preterites and participles of verbs in URL and IRL.

ORM.
As in *form*. Rhymes storm, conform, deform, inform, perform, reform, misinform, uniform, multiform, warm, swarm, chloroform, transform.
As in *worm*. See ERM.

ORN.
Born, corn, morn, horn, scorn, thorn, adorn, suborn, unicorn, sorn, capricorn, shorn, torn, worn, lorn, forlorn, lovelorn, sworn, foresworn, overborne, foreborne, mourn, warn, forewarn.

ORP.
Thorp, warp.

ORPS.
Corps rhymes ORE.

ORPSE.
Corpse rhymes plurals of nouns and preterites and participles of verbs in ARP.

ORSE.

Horse, endorse, unhorse, force, remorse, coarse, course, torse, morse, corse.

ORST.

See URST.

ORT.

Short, sort, exhort, consort, distort, extort, resort, retort, snort, mort, wart, fort, port, court, report, morte, wart, thwart, quart, swart.

ORTS.

Orts, plural of nouns and third person singular present of verbs in ORT.

ORTH.

As in *north*. Rhymes fourth.
As in *worth*. See ERTH.

OSE.

As in *jocose*. Rhymes close, dose, morose, gross, engross, verbose.

As in *pose*. Rhymes close, dose, hose, chose, glose, froze, nose, prose, those, rose, compose, depose, disclose, dispose, discompose, expose, impose, enclose, interpose, oppose, propose, recompose, repose, suppose, transpose, arose, presuppose, foreclose, gloze,

etc., and the plurals of nouns and apostrophized preterites and participles of verbs in Ow, Oe, O.
As in *lose*. See Use.

OSH.
Bosh, wash, swash.

OSM.
Microcosm, no rhyme.

OSQUE, OSK.
Mosque, kiosk.

OSS.
Boss, cross, dross, moss, loss, across, albatross, doss, emboss.

OST.
As in *cost*. Rhymes frost, lost, accost, holocaust, etc., and the preterites and participles of words in Oss.

As in *ghost*. Rhymes post, most, coast, and second person singular present of verbs in Ow, as ow'st.

As in *dost*. See Ust.

OT.
Clot, cot, blot, got, hot, jot, lot, knot, not, plot, pot, scot, shot, polyglot, sot, spot, apricot, trot, rot, grot, begot, forgot, allot, complot, yacht, quat, melilot, counterplot, what.

OTCH.

Botch, notch, crotch, blotch, Scotch, watch.

OTE.

Note, vote, lote, mote, quote, rote, wrote, smote, denote, tote, promote, remote, devote, anecdote, antidote, boat, coat, bloat, doat, float, gloat, goat, oat, overfloat, afloat, throat, moat.

OTH.

As in *broth*. Rhymes cloth, froth, troth, wrath.
As in *both*. Rhymes loth, sloth, oath, growth, both, loath.
As in *moth*. Rhymes cloth.

OTHE.

Clothe, loathe (with *s* added rhymes *oaths;* though *clothes*, the noun, in comic verse may rhyme with *snows*, being colloquially spoken *clo's*).

OU.

As in *thou*. See Ow.
As in *you*. See Ew.

OUBT.

Doubt, see OUT.

OUC.

See OOK.

OUCH.

As in *couch*. Pouch, vouch, slouch, avouch, crouch.
As in *touch*. See UTCH.

OUCHE.

Cartouche, buche.

OUD.

Shroud, cloud, loud, proud, aloud, crowd, o'ershroud, etc., and the preterites and participles of verbs in Ow.

OUGH.

Has various pronunciations. See OFF, OW, OWE, OCK, O, EW, and UFF.

OUGE.

As in *rouge*. Rhymes gamboge.

OUGHT.

Bought, thought, ought, brought, forethought, fought, nought, sought, wrought, besought, bethought, methought, aught, naught, caught, taught.

OUL.

As in *foul*. See OWL.
As in *soul*. See OLE.

OULD.

Mould, fold, old, cold, and the preterites and participles of verbs in OWL, OLL, and OLE.

OULT.

See OLT.

OUN.

See OWN.

OUNCE.

Bounce, flounce, renounce, pounce, ounce, denounce, pronounce.

OUND.

As in *bound*. Rhymes found, mound, ground, hound, pound, round, sound, wound (verb), abound, aground, around, confound, compound, expound, profound, rebound, resound, propound, surround, etc., and the preterites and participles of verbs in OWN.

As in *wound*—the noun. Rhymes preterites and participles of verbs in OON, UNE.

OUNG.

See UNG.

OUNT.

Count, mount, fount, amount, dismount, remount, surmount, account, discount, miscount, account.

OUP.

See OOP.

OUPH, or OUPHE.

Ouphe, or ouph. See Oof.

OUQUE.

Chibouque. See Uke.

OUR.

As in *hour*. Rhymes lour, sour, our, scour, deflow'r, devour, bow'r, tow'r, etc.
As in *pour*. See Ore.
As in *tour*. See Ure.

OURGE.

See Urge.

OURN.

As in *adjourn*. See Urn.
As in *mourn*. See Orn.

OURNE.

Bourne, rhymes Orn.

OURS.

As in *ours*. Rhymes the plurals of nouns and third persons singular present tense of verbs in Our and Ow'r.

As in *yours*. Rhymes the plurals of nouns and third persons singular present tense of verbs in Ure, Oor, etc.

OURSE.
Course. See ORSE.

OURT.
Court. See ORT.

OURTH.
Fourth. See ORTH.

OUS.
Nous, house, mouse, chouse, douse.

OUSE.
As in *house* (noun). See OUS.
As in *spouse*. See OWZE.

OUST.
Joust, Faust.

OUT.
Bout, stout, out, clout, pout, gout, grout, rout, scout, shout, tout, snout, spout, stout, sprout, trout, about, devout, without, throughout, doubt, redoubt, misdoubt, drought.

OUTH.
As in *mouth* (noun). Rhymes south, drouth.
As in *youth*. See UTH.
As in *mouth* (verb), no rhyme.

OVE.

As in *wove.* Rhymes inwove, interwove, hove, alcove, clove, grove, behove, rove, stove, strove, throve, drove.

As in *dove.* Rhymes love, shove, glove, above.

As in *move.* Rhymes approve, disprove, disapprove, improve, groove, prove, reprove.

OW.

As in *now.* Rhymes bow, how, mow, cow, brow, sow, vow, prow, avow, allow, trow, disallow, endow, bough, plough, slough (mire), thou.

As in *blow.* See O.

OWD.

Crowd. See OUD.

OWE.

Owe. See OW.

OWL.

As in *cowl.* Rhymes growl, owl, fowl, howl, prowl, scowl, etc.

As in *bowl.* See OLE.

OWN.

As in *brown.* Rhymes town, clown, crown, down, drown, frown, gown, adown, renown, embrown, noun.

As in *thrown.* See ONE.

OWSE.

Bowse, rouse. See OUSE.

OWTH.
Growth. See OTH.

OWZE.
Blowze, browse, rouse, spouse, carouse, touse, espouse, the verbs to house, mouse, etc., and the plurals of nouns and third persons singular present tense of verbs in OW.

OX.
Ox, box, fox, equinox, orthodox, heterodox, the plurals of nouns and third persons singular present tense of verbs in OCK.

OY.
Boy, buoy, coy, employ, cloy, joy, toy, alloy, annoy, convoy, decoy, destroy, enjoy, employ.

OYNT.
Aroynt. See OINT.

OYLE.
Scroyle. See OIL.

OYNE.
Royne. See OIN.

OZ.
As in *poz*. Rhymes was.
As in *coz*. See UZ.

OZE.
See OSE.

U

U.
See Ew.

UB.
Cub, club, dub, chub, drub, grub, hub, rub, snub, shrub, tub.

UBE.
Cube, tube.

UCE.
Truce, sluice, spruce, deuce, conduce, deduce, induce, introduce, puce, produce, seduce, traduce, juice, reduce, use, abuse, profuse, abstruse, disuse, excuse, misuse, obtuse, recluse.

UCH.
See Utch.

UCK.
Buck, luck, pluck, suck, struck, tuck, truck, duck.

UCT.
Conduct, deduct, instruct, obstruct, aqueduct. The preterites and participles of verbs in Uck.

UD.
Bud, scud, stud, mud, cud, blood, flood. [Su.. rhymes plurals of nouns and third person present singular of verbs in Ud.]

UDE.

Rude, crude, prude, allude, conclude, delude, elude, include, mood, food, rood, illude, exclude, exude, snood, include, intrude, obtrude, seclude, altitude, fortitude, gratitude, interlude, latitude, longitude, magnitude, multitude, solicitude, solitude, vicissitude, aptitude, habitude, ingratitude, inaptitude, lassitude, plenitude, promptitude, servitude, similitude, lewd, feud, brood, and the preterites and participles of verbs in EW, UE, etc.

UDGE.

Judge, drudge, grudge, trudge, adjudge, prejudge, fudge, smudge, nudge, budge, sludge.

UE.

See Ew.

UFF.

Buff, cuff, chuff, bluff, huff, gruff, luff, puff, snuff stuff, ruff, rebuff, counterbuff, rough, tough, enough, slough (cast skin), chough.

UFT.

Tuft rhymes the preterites and participles of verbs in UFF.

UG.

Lug, bug, dug, drug, hug, jug, rug, slug, smug, snug, mug, shrug, pug.

UGUE.

Fugue, no rhyme.

UHL.
See ULE.

UICE.
See USE.

UIDE.
See IDE.

UILD.
See ILD.

UILT.
See ILT.

UINT.
See INT.

UISE.
As in *guise*. See ISE.
As in *bruise*. See USE.

UISH.
Cuish. See ISH.

UIT.
See UTE.

UKE.
Duke, puke, rebuke, fluke, chibouque.

UL, and ULL.
As in *cull*. Rhymes dull, gull, hull, lull, mull, null, trull, skull, annul, disannul.
As in *full*. Rhymes wool, bull, pull, bountiful, fan-

ciful, sorrowful, dutiful, merciful, wonderful, worshiprul, and every word ending in ful having the accent on the ante-penultimate.

ULCH.

Mulch, gulch.

ULE.

Mule, pule, Yule, rule, overrule, ridicule, misrule, fool, tool, buhl. (Gules, heraldic term, rhymes plural of nouns and third person singular present of verbs in ULE, etc.)

ULF.

Gulf, no rhyme.

ULGE.

Bulge, indulge, divulge, etc.

ULK.

Bulk, hulk, skulk, sulk.

ULM.

Culm, no rhyme.

ULP.

Gulp, sculp, pulp, ensculp.

ULSE.

Pulse, repulse, impulse, expulse, convulse, insulse.

ULT.

Result, adult, exult, consult, indult, occult, insult, difficult, catapult, etc.

UM.

Crum, chum, drum, glum, gum, hum, mum, scum, plum, sum, swum, thrum, thumb, dumb, succumb, come, become, overcome, burdensome, cumbersome, frolicsome, humorsome, quarrelsome, troublesome, encomium, opium, crumb.

UMB.

See UM.

UME.

See OOM.

UMP.

Bump, pump, jump, lump, plump, rump, stump, trump, thump, clump.

UN.

Dun, gun, nun, pun, run, sun, shun, tun, stun, spun, begun, son, won, ton, done, one, none, undone, bun.

UNCE.

Dunce, once.

UNCH.

Bunch, punch, hunch, lunch, munch, scrunch, crunch.

UNCT.

Defunct, disjunct, rhyme preterites and participles of verbs in UNK.

UND.

Fund, refund, preterites of verbs in UN.

UNE.

June, tune, untune, jejune, prune, croon, hewn, swoon, moon, soon, boon, noon, spoon, buffoon, lampoon, poltroon, triune, 'coon, cocoon, raccoon, dune, shalloon, dragoon.

UNG.

Bung, clung, dung, flung, hung, rung, strung, sung, sprung, slung, stung, swung, wrung, unsung, young, tongue, among.

UNGE.

Plunge, sponge, expunge.

UNK.

Drunk, bunk, hunk, sunk, shrunk, stunk, punk, trunk, slunk, funk, chunk, monk. (Hunks rhymes plural of nouns and third person singular present of verbs in UNK.)

UNT.

Brunt, blunt, hunt, runt, grunt, front, etc., and (?) wont (to be accustomed).

UOR.
See ORE.

UP.
Cup, sup, pup, dup, up.

UPT.
Abrupt, corrupt, interrupt, the participles and preterites of verbs in UP, etc.

UR.
See ER.

URB.
Curb, disturb, verb, herb.

URCH.
Church, lurch, birch, perch, search, smirch.

URD.
Curd, absurd, bird, gird, heard, herd, sherd, word, and the preterites and participles of verbs in ER, UR, and IR.

URE.
Cure, pure, dure, lure, sure, abjure, allure, assure, demure, conjure, endure, manure, inure, insure, immature, immure, mature, obscure, procure, secure, adjure, calenture, coverture, epicure, investiture, forfeiture, furniture, miniature, nourriture, overture, portraiture, primogeniture, temperature, poor, moor, contour, amour, your.

URF.
Turf, scurf, serf, surf.

URGE.
Purge, urge, surge, scourge, thaumaturge, gurge, verge, diverge.

URK.
Lurk, Turk, work, irk, jerk, perk, quirk, mirk.

URL.
Churl, curl, furl, hurl, purl, uncurl, unfurl, whirl, earl, girl, twirl, pearl.

URM.
See ERM.

URN.
Burn, churn, spurn, turn, urn, return, overturn, tern, discern, earn, sojourn, adjourn, rejourn.

URP.
Usurp, chirp, extirp, discerp.

URR.
Purr. See UR.

URSE.
See ERSE.

URST.
Burst, curst, durst, accurst, thirst, worst, first, versed.

URT.
See ERT.

US, or USS.

Pus, us, thus, buss, truss, discuss, incubus, overplus, arquebus, cuss, amorous, boisterous, clamorous, credulous, dangerous, ungenerous, generous, emulous, fabulous, frivolous, hazardous, idolatrous, infamous, miraculous, mischievous, mountainous, mutinous, necessitous, numerous, ominous, perilous, poisonous, populous, prosperous, ridiculous, riotous, ruinous, scandalous, scrupulous, sedulous, traitorous, treacherous, tyrannous, venomous, vigorous, villanous, adventurous, adulterous, ambiguous, blasphemous, dolorous, fortuitous, gluttonous, gratuitous, incredulous, lecherous, libidinous, magnanimous, obstreperous, odoriferous, ponderous, ravenous, rigorous, slanderous, solicitous, timorous, valorous, unanimous, calamitous.

USE.

As in the noun *use*. Rhymes disuse, abuse, deuce, truce, sluice, juice, loose, goose, noose, moose.

As in *muse*. Rhymes the verb use, abuse, lose, choose, shoes, amuse, diffuse, excuse, infuse, misuse, peruse, refuse, suffuse, transfuse, accuse, bruise, and the plurals of nouns and third persons singular of verbs in Ew and UE, etc.

USH.

As in *blush*. Rhymes brush, crush, gush, flush, rush, lush, tush, frush, hush.

As in *bush*. Rhymes push.

USK.

Busk, tusk, dusk, husk, musk.

USP.
Cusp, no rhyme.

UST.
Bust, crust, dust, just, must, lust, rust, thrust, trust, adjust, disgust, distrust, intrust, mistrust, robust, unjust, the preterites and participles of verbs in US, USS, etc.

UT, or UTT.
But, butt, cut, hut, gut, glut, jut, nut, shut, strut, englut, rut, scut, slut, smut, abut, and soot (?).

UTCH.
Hutch, crutch, Dutch, much, such, touch.

UTE.
Brute, lute, flute, mute, acute, compute, confute, dispute, dilute, depute, impute, minute, pollute, refute, salute, absolute, attribute, contribute, constitute, destitute, dissolute, execute, institute, persecute, prosecute, resolute, substitute, fruit, bruit, suit, recruit, boot, hoot, coot, shoot, toot, soot (?).

UTH.
As in *azimuth*. Rhymes doth.
As in *truth*. See OOTH.

UX.
Dux, crux, lux, flux, reflux. The plurals of nouns and third persons singular of verbs in UCK.

Y

Y.
See IE.

YB.
Syb. See IB.

YM.
Sym. See IM.

YMN.
Hymn. See IM.

YMPH.
Nymph, lymph.

YN.
Baudekyn. See IN.

YNE.
Anodyne. See INE.

YNX.
Lynx rhymes plurals of nouns and third persons present singular of verbs in INK.

YP.
Gyp, hyp. See IP.

YPE.
Type. See IPE.

YPH.
Hieroglyph. See IFF.

YPSE.
Apocalypse. See IPSE.

YRE.
See IRE.

YRRH.
See UR.

YSM.
See ISM.

YST.
See IST.

YVE.
Gyve. See IVE.

YX.
Sardonyx, pyx, fix, rhyme plural of nouns and third persons singular present of verbs in ICK.

YZE.
Analyze. See ISE.

THE END.

www.ingramcontent.com/pod-product-compliance
Lightning Source LLC
Chambersburg PA
CBHW020330170426
43200CB00006B/335